Contents

How to use this book

As Principal Examiners for the WJEC Chemistry specification we have written this study guide to help you be aware of what is required so that you succeed in the GCE examination. The book is divided into two main sections: for CH4 and for CH5.

Knowledge and Understanding

The first part of each section covers the key knowledge that is required for the examination.

In addition, we have given you additional pointers to help you develop your learning:

- There are 'Quickfire' questions designed to test your knowledge and understanding of the material.
- There are 'Grade Boost' tips – these often outline weaknesses that we have seen in actual papers.

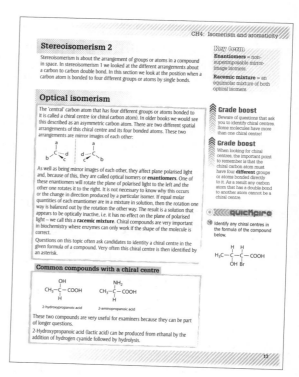

Illuminate
Publishing

WJEC
A2 Chemistry

Study and Revision Guide

David Ballard • Rhodri Thomas

ip

Published in 2012 by Illuminate Publishing Ltd, P.O Box 1160, Cheltenham, Gloucestershire GL50 9RW

Orders: Please visit www.illuminatepublishing.com
or email sales@illuminatepublishing.com

British Library Cataloguing in Publication Data

A catalogue record for this book is available from the British Library

ISBN 978-0-9568401-8-9

Printed by T J International, Padstow, Cornwall

The publisher's policy is to use papers that are natural, renewable and recyclable products made from wood grown in sustainable forests. The logging and manufacturing processes are expected to conform to the environmental regulations of the country of origin.

Every effort has been made to contact copyright holders of material reproduced in this book. If notified, the publishers will be pleased to rectify any errors or omissions at the earliest opportunity.

This material has been endorsed by WJEC and offers high quality support for the delivery of WJEC qualifications. While this material has been through a WJEC quality assurance process, all responsibility for the content remains with the publisher.

Editor: Geoff Tuttle

Design and layout: Nigel Harriss

Acknowledgements

We are very grateful to the team at Illuminate Publishing for their professionalism, support and guidance throughout this project. It has been a pleasure to work so closely with them.

The authors and publisher wish to thank:

Judith Bonello for her thorough review of the book and expert insights and observations.

Jonathan Owen of WJEC.

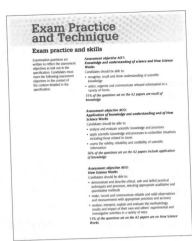

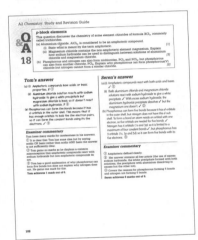

Exam Practice and Technique

The second part of each section covers the key skills needed for examination success and gives examples of responses to examination questions. We begin by giving you an insight into the examination itself and how it is assessed.

A variety of questions are provided – most of these are structured style questions with a few longer answer questions. This reflects the form of the examination. Each question presents you with two typical candidate answers with comments about their performance. Each question in the CH4 section ranges over a number of topics – as in the paper. The questions in the CH5 section are more focused on individual topics – as reflected in the examination questions.

We advise you to seek out and learn from a number of sources and not to just rely on a particular book and the notes from your teachers.

You will find detailed revision guides for each unit on the WJEC website www.wjec.co.uk but you should be selective when using this material and refer to your specification at all times. Remember to take advantage of the range of past papers (and their mark schemes) available.

We hope that you find this little book useful in your studies and that it helps you to gain the grades that will enable you to advance to the next level of your career.

David Ballard and Rhodri Thomas

Knowledge and Understanding

CH4 Analysing and Building Molecules

The CH4 unit builds on the foundation ideas of spectroscopy and basic organic chemistry introduced at AS level and goes on to explore these concepts in more detail. Modern organic chemistry relies for its understanding on the mechanistic background to reactions which, in turn, closely link to polarity in bonds – particularly bonds between atoms of carbon, hydrogen, oxygen, nitrogen and halogens. Finding the structure of organic compounds now depends much more on infrared and NMR spectroscopy and also mass spectrometry, rather than the more traditional elemental analysis and functional group reactions. The latter though, do still have an important role and this is explored in the various topics in this unit.

Revision checklist

Tick column 1 when you have completed brief revision notes.
Tick column 2 when you think you have a good grasp of the topic.
Tick column 3 during your final revision for the examination and when you feel that you have mastered the material in the topic.

		1	2	3	Notes
	Spectroscopy				
p8	Colour in organic compounds				
p9	Groups responsible for colour in organic compounds				
	Isomerism and aromaticity				
p10	How to name the aliphatic organic compounds in this unit	✓			
p12	Stereoisomerism 1: E–Z isomerism	✓			
p13	Stereoisomerism 2: Optical isomerism	✓			
p14	The structure of benzene	✓			
p15	The nitration, halogenation and alkylation of benzene	✓			
p17	The alkaline hydrolysis of chloroalkanes and chlorobenzene	✓			

		1	2	3	Notes
Organic compounds containing oxygen					
p18	Forming primary and secondary alcohols	✓			
p19	The production of esters and alkenes from alcohols	✓			
p20	The oxidation of primary and secondary alcohols	✓			
p21	The reactions of phenol	✓			
p22	Identifying aldehydes and ketones	✓			
p24	The addition of hydrogen cyanide to carbonyl compounds	✓			
p25	Physical properties of carboxylic acids	✓			
p26	The relative acidities of carboxylic acids, phenol, alcohols and water	✓			
p27	Forming carboxylic acids by oxidation	✓			
p29	Forming acid chlorides from carboxylic acids and their reactions	✓			
Organic compounds containing nitrogen					
p30	Making and reacting nitriles	✓			
p31	Making and reacting aliphatic and aromatic amines	✓			
p33	α-Amino acids and proteins				
Organic synthesis and analysis					
p35	Empirical and molecular formulae	✓			
p36	Using mass, IR and NMR data in structure determination	✓			
p39	Basic practical techniques in organic chemistry				
p42	Organic conversions and yields				
p44	Polymer chemistry				
How science works					
p46	The work of scientists – methods and validity				

Spectroscopy

Spectroscopic techniques have become very important in the determination of the structure of organic compounds, as well as in assessing their purity.

The electromagnetic spectrum shows a gradation in energy and frequency across the various regions. In this unit we are particularly concerned with the infrared and visible regions, together with the radio wave region for NMR spectra. You will have already met infrared spectra and mass spectroscopy in the AS revision guide. More details about infrared and NMR spectra occur later in this guide.

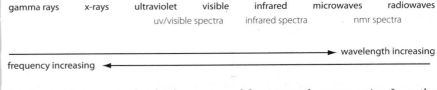

gamma rays	x-rays	ultraviolet	visible	infrared	microwaves	radiowaves
		uv/visible spectra		infrared spectra	nmr spectra	

→ wavelength increasing

frequency increasing ←

It is important to note that both energy and frequency decrease; going from the ultraviolet through visible to the infrared region. Thus, blue light is of a higher energy than red light. As frequency gets smaller and therefore wavelength increases, blue light must have a shorter wavelength than red light.

	violet	blue	green	yellow	orange	red	
	4.00	4.50	5.00	5.80	6.00	7.00	wavelength / $\times 10^{-7}$ m

→ wavelength increasing

frequency increasing ←

energy increasing ←

Colour in organic compounds

We often think of organic compounds as 'boring' colourless liquids or white crystalline solids but in fact a number are coloured – just think of the many flowers in our gardens and the colours that are used to dye our clothes. The colour that we see is the colour that is **not** being absorbed by the compound to excite its electrons. In spring we see bluebells in our woodland. Each flower is absorbing light at the red end of the visible spectrum. Since blue light is not being absorbed, we see the flower as blue. Similarly the flowers of red roses must be absorbing light at the blue end of the visible region of the electromagnetic spectrum.

Many organic compounds absorb ultraviolet light but, of course, our eyes are not able to detect the ultraviolet spectrum and so we just see the compound as white or colourless. A number of insects, though, are sensitive to changes in the ultraviolet region.

>> *Pointer*

It is quite common for candidates to muddle up frequency and wavelength.

Frequency is measured in Hertz, and wavelength in metres.

Remember – the shorter the wavelength, the higher the frequency.

quickfire

① Gareth says that a red rose flower appears black when seen in blue light.

Explain why he is correct.

quickfire

② Chlorophyll is responsible for the green colour in leaves.

What colour or colours must it be absorbing in sunlight?

Groups responsible for colour in organic compounds

The formulae for some coloured organic compounds are shown below:

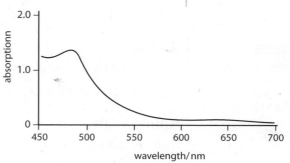

ethanedial
yellow

nitrobenzene
yellow

l,2-benzoquinone red

l,2-diphenylethanedione yellow

All of these compounds contain a group or series of groups that are responsible for the compound being coloured. Such groups are called chromophores. A single group is often not able to produce colour in a compound by itself. The compound generally has to have several of these groups for it to have a colour.

colourless

yellow green

Very often the single group has a double bond (e.g. C=C, C=O or N=N) and is separated from similar groups by single covalent bonds. This repeating pattern of double and single bonds is called **conjugation**.

Here is the formula and the visible spectrum of the orange compound β-carotene, founds in carrots and a commonly used, and safe, food colouring agent:

You will see that β-carotene contains an extensive conjugated system of single and double carbon to carbon bonds. Since its absorption maximum is at about 480 ᴨm, it absorbs blue light and is seen as orange.

absorption

2.0 –

1.0 –

0 –

450   500   550   600   650   700

wavelength/nm

Key Term

Conjugation = a repeating pattern of single and double bonds between carbon atoms.

》 Pointer

Many azo dyes contain a benzene ring bonded to a –N=N– group as the chromophore.

⊙》《《《 quickfire

③ A biological stain has an absorption maximum at 510 nm.

State its colour, giving reasons for your answer.

Isomerism and aromaticity

How to name the aliphatic organic compounds in this unit

You will know that many organic compounds have traditional names, particularly those materials that have been in common use for many years. We are familiar with acetic acid found in vinegar. However, to continue to use this system has meant learning names that did not help us derive the formula, and a systematic way of naming organic compounds has been developed. In this unit you are asked to extend the naming learnt in CH2 to include the additional classes of compounds that you are learning about.

Aldehydes and ketones

The systematic name of an aldehyde ends in –al and for a ketone, –one.

CH_3CHO ethanal CH_3COCH_3 propanone

Carboxylic acids

As might be expected, the systematic name ends in –oic acid.

HCOOH   methanoic acid $ClCH_2CH_2CH_2COOH$ 4-chlorobutanoic acid

Esters

These are tricky to name – the alkyl group (from the alcohol) is named first and then the 'acid' part, ending in –oate.

$CH_3CH_2COOCH_3$ methyl propanoate $HCOOCH_2CH_3$ ethyl methanoate

Acid (or acyl) chlorides

Think of its parent carboxylic acid, remove '-oic acid' and add 'oyl chloride'

CH_3COCl is derived from ethanoic acid and is named 'ethanoyl chloride'.

Amides (or carboxylic acid amides)

Think of its parent carboxylic acid, remove '-oic acid' and add 'amide'.

$CH_3CH_2CONH_2$ is named propanamide.

Amines

These are simply named after the carbon chain with 'amine' at the end.

CH_3NH_2 methylamine $CH_3CH(CH_3)CH_2NH_2$ is 2-methylpropylamine

Amino acids

These are named after the parent carboxylic acid with 'amino' added.

$CH_3CH(NH_2)COOH$ 2-aminopropanoic acid   (alanine)

>> **Pointer**

Beware – very often the structural formulae of esters are written backwards with the 'acid part' first – the opposite way round to its name.

 quickfire

④ The name for the formula below is ethanedial:

OHC-CHO

Can you see why this is?

Grade boost

It is important to write the atoms in functional groups in the correct order. For example, CH_3COH is an incorrect formula for ethanal and will lose marks.

Unit CH4 contains the chemistry of compounds containing benzene rings, these are called aromatic compounds. Some of these compounds have traditional names, for example aniline, but these do not give any indication of the structure of the compound. A systematic system has been developed to name aromatic compounds based on benzene, with a few exceptions. The carbon atoms of the ring are numbered, with the lowest numbering used wherever possible. The 'main' functional group is usually in the 1-position. Sometimes the ring is not drawn and, for example, chlorobenzene is simply given as C_6H_5Cl.

Examples named after benzene

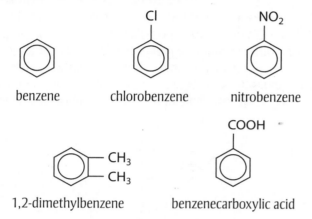

benzene   chlorobenzene   nitrobenzene

1,2-dimethylbenzene   benzenecarboxylic acid

Examples not following the general rule

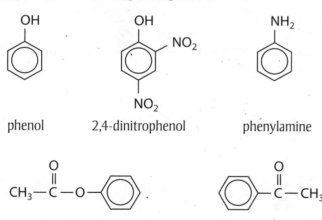

phenol   2,4-dinitrophenol   phenylamine

phenyl ethanoate   phenylethanone

>> **Pointer**

It is quite common for examiners to see 'di' missed out when naming compounds. For example, instead of 1,3-dimethylbenzene, candidates write just 1,3-methylbenzene. This would be marked wrong.

quickfire

⑤ The correct name for the explosive picric acid is 2,4,6-trinitrophenol.

See if you can write its structure.

quickfire

⑥ An acid-base indicator has the molecular formula $C_6H_6N_1O_3$.

It is a phenol with a nitro group in the 4-position. Give its structural formula.

quickfire

⑦ Write the structural formula of any aromatic isomer of ethylbenzene.

Grade boost

Be very careful when describing stereoisomerism. It is incorrect to say that 'stereoisomers have the same molecular or empirical formulae but differ in the spatial arrangement of their atoms'.

Compounds with the same molecular or empirical formulae are not necessarily in the same family of compounds.

Grade boost

If you are asked to explain why E–Z isomerism occurs, beware of writing 'because the double bond cannot rotate'. Of course it can completely rotate, but the important point is that one end cannot rotate relative to the other end.

quickfire

⑧ Draw the structural formula of pent-1-ene and state why this compound cannot show E–Z isomerism.

quickfire

⑨ Draw the structural formula of (Z)-but-2-ene.

Stereoisomerism 1

Stereoisomerism is about how atoms and groups are arranged in space. As the name suggests, stereoisomers must be isomers that differ in some way because of their spatial arrangement. They must have the same structural formula (arrangement of atoms) but differ in the way the bonds are arranged in space.

There are two forms of stereoisomerism: E–Z isomerism and optical isomerism.

E–Z isomerism

You will have met E–Z isomerism before at AS level but it also occurs in this unit. Compounds showing this type of isomerism have at least one carbon to carbon double bond with different atoms or groups bonded to these carbon atoms. These atoms or groups can be the same or different but there cannot be two identical atoms or groups the same bonded to the same carbon atom. The simplest illustration is one where each 'end' of the double bond has the same atoms or groups:

(E)– 1,2–dichloroethene   (Z)– 1,2–dichloroethene

If the two atoms or groups are 'opposite' each other, then it is the E-isomer and if they are not opposite each other then it is called the Z-isomer.

Of course it is not necessary to have the atoms or groups the same. Let us look at the stereoisomers of 1-bromo-2-chloropropene, $CH_3CCl=CHBr$. These can be drawn as the E- or the Z- forms:

(E)–1–bromo–2–chloropropene   (Z)–1–bromo–2–chloropropene

These are obviously stereoisomers, as the atoms/groups have different spatial arrangements. There are rules for deciding which of the two is the E-isomer and which one is the Z-isomer but this detail is not required at A2 level. The naming of these type of compounds will not be expected.

Until recently this type of isomerism was called geometrical isomerism and the E-isomerism was 'trans' and the Z-isomer the 'cis' form.

Sometimes examination questions ask 'why does this type of stereoisomerism occur?' One end of the double bond cannot rotate relative to its other end – strictly, an acceptable form of words is 'there is no rotation about a double bond'.

Stereoisomerism 2

Stereoisomerism is about the arrangement of groups or atoms in a compound in space. In stereoisomerism 1 we looked at the different arrangements about a carbon to carbon double bond. In this section we look at the position when a carbon atom is bonded to four different groups or atoms by single bonds.

Optical isomerism

The 'central' carbon atom that has four different groups or atoms bonded to it is called a chiral centre (or chiral carbon atom). In older books we would see this described as an asymmetric carbon atom. There are two different spatial arrangements of this chiral centre and its four bonded atoms. These two arrangements are mirror images of each other:

As well as being mirror images of each other, they affect plane polarised light and, because of this, they are called optical isomers or **enantiomers**. One of these enantiomers will rotate the plane of polarised light to the left and the other one rotates it to the right. It is not necessary to know why this occurs or the change in direction produced by a particular isomer. If equal molar quantities of each enantiomer are in a mixture in solution, then the rotation one way is balanced out by the rotation the other way. The result is a solution that appears to be optically inactive, i.e. it has no effect on the plane of polarised light – we call this a **racemic mixture**. Chiral compounds are very important in biochemistry where enzymes can only work if the shape of the molecule is correct.

Questions on this topic often ask candidates to identity a chiral centre in the given formula of a compound. Very often this chiral centre is then identified by an asterisk.

Common compounds with a chiral centre

2-hydroxypropanoic acid

2-aminopropanoic acid

These two compounds are very useful for examiners because they can be part of longer questions.

2-Hydroxypropanoic acid (lactic acid) can be produced from ethanal by the addition of hydrogen cyanide followed by hydrolysis.

Key term

Enantiomers = non-superimposable mirror-image isomers.

Racemic mixture = an equimolar mixture of both optical isomers.

Grade boost

Beware of questions that ask you to identify chiral centres. Some molecules have more than one chiral centre!

Grade boost

When looking for chiral centres, the important point to remember is that the chiral carbon atom must have four **different** groups or atoms bonded directly to it. As a result any carbon atom that has a double bond to another atom cannot be a chiral centre.

quickfire

⑩ Identify any chiral centres in the formula of the compound below.

$$H_3C - \overset{\overset{\displaystyle H}{|}}{C} - \overset{\overset{\displaystyle H}{|}}{\underset{\underset{\displaystyle Br}{|}}{C}} - COOH$$
$$\underset{\displaystyle OH}{|}$$

Key Term

Delocalisation = electron pairs are shared between three or more carbon atoms, as in aromatic compounds such as benzene and naphthalene.

» Pointer

Although benzene does not react with bromine water (aqueous bromine), more reactive aromatic compounds will react with it. However, these lead to substitution products not addition products.

Grade boost

Three pieces of evidence for the delocalised structure of benzene are:

- All bond lengths are the same.
- The enthalpy of hydrogenation means that benzene is more stable than suggested by the Kekulé structure.
- Benzene tends to react by substitution rather than by addition.

The structure of benzene

The molecular formula of benzene is C_6H_6 and X-ray studies show that the carbon atoms form a flat hexagon with the C-C-C bond angle 120°. The Kekulé structure of benzene shows an alternating system of single and double carbon to carbon bonds around the ring. However, if this was true, benzene would decolourise bromine water, like an alkene, and this does not happen. It would also be a reactive compound, which it is not.

Kekulé form   delocalised form

Evidence suggests that benzene contains a **delocalised** electron structure with a π-cloud of electrons around the ring. Support for this is that each carbon to carbon bond has the same length and that this is intermediate in size between the lengths of the double and single bonds.

The delocalisation energy of benzene

The reaction of cyclohexene (a six-membered ring with one carbon to carbon double bond) with hydrogen to produce cyclohexane, gives out 120 kJ mol^{-1} ($\Delta H_{hydrogenation} = -120$ kJ mol^{-1}). A similar hydrogenation of cyclohexa-1,3-diene to produce cyclohexane produces -240 kJ mol^{-1}. If benzene contained three double bonds (the Kekulé structure) then we would expect a value of around -360 kJ mol^{-1}, when cyclohexane is made by hydrogenation. In fact the value turns out to be -208 kJ mol^{-1}. This figure suggests that benzene does **not** have the Kekulé structure and is more stable than the alternating double bond – single bond structure. The difference between the 'expected' and found values (152 kJ mol^{-1}) is called the delocalisation (or resonance) energy. These energy values provide further evidence for the delocalised structure of benzene.

The resistance of benzene to addition reactions

Alkenes react mainly by addition, for example the hydrogenation of propene to give propane:

$$CH_3CH=CH_2 \ + \ H_2 \ \rightarrow \ CH_3CH_2CH_3$$

and the reaction of ethene with hydrogen chloride to give chloroethane:

$$CH_2=CH_2 \ + \ HCl \ \rightarrow \ CH_3CH_2Cl$$

However, benzene finds it difficult to react by addition. This is more evidence in favour of the stable delocalised electron ring structure. If addition occurred then the stable π-electron cloud would be lost. The preferred way for benzene to react is by the substitution of the hydrogen atoms, as this would retain the delocalised structure of the molecule.

The nitration, halogenation and alkylation of benzene

Benzene usually reacts by substitution so that stability of the π-electron ring system is maintained. Since the π-cloud of electrons is negatively charged, the most common reaction of benzene involves **electrophilic substitution**. The 'incoming' group needs to be an electrophile and this is usually made from the reactants '*in situ*' – this means that it is made and reacts as it is formed.

The nitration of benzene

Nitrobenzene, $C_6H_5NO_2$, is made by reacting benzene with a mixture of concentrated nitric and sulfuric acids at 50°C or below. If the temperature rises above this then some dinitration can occur – giving 1,3-dinitrobenzene, which is a pale yellow solid.

The equation for making the electrophile NO_2^+ (the nitronium ion, sometimes called the nitryl cation) from the acids is not needed, but the mechanism showing how the nitronium ion reacts with benzene is an essential part of revision!

The halogenation of benzene

Bromobenzene, C_6H_5Br, is made from benzene and bromine in the presence of a catalyst at room temperature. The catalyst often used is iron(III) bromide, although books may list other suitable materials. Sometimes the catalyst is described as a 'halogen carrier' and this would be acceptable in an examination answer. You will often find books describing the reaction as being done in the dark – but, of course, if this was taken literally you would not be able to see what is going on! The correct description is probably 'out of direct sunlight'.

Key Term

Electrophilic substitution = replacement of 'ring hydrogen atoms' by an electron-deficient 'group' such as NO_2^+ or CH_3^+.

quickfire

⑪ 0.1 mole of benzene is completely nitrated to give only nitrobenzene.

What is the mass of nitrobenzene produced?

[A_r: H = 1; C = 12; N = 14; O = 16]

>> *Pointer*

Strong sunlight is not advisable for this reaction as the ultraviolet light may encourage an addition reaction between benzene and the halogen.

Key Term

Polarisation = an unequal electron distribution in a covalent bond.

quickfire

⑫ A scientist reacted 0.20 mole of benzene with bromine. He obtained 24.0 g of bromobenzene (M_r 157).

Calculate the percentage yield of bromobenzene.

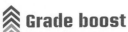

Grade boost

When writing mechanisms always check that the curly arrow is coming from the benzene ring and not from the nitro-group or bromine atom. It is a common error to write it the other way round.

As with the nitration of benzene, this halogenation is an electrophilic substitution reaction. The catalyst causes **polarisation** of the Br–Br bond followed by reaction with the benzene ring:

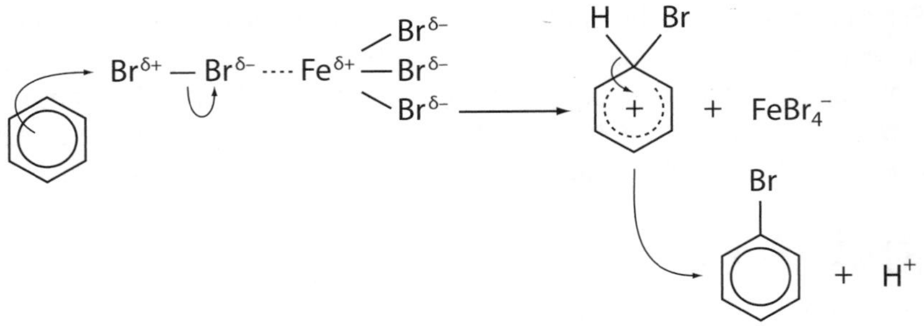

The two ions formed H^+ and $FeBr_4^-$ can then react together to give hydrogen bromide gas and iron(III) bromide. Hydrogen bromide gas is lost from the reaction mixture – hence the need for the reaction to be carried out in a fume cupboard. The iron(III) bromide can then carry out the reaction again – hence its 'catalytic' action.

If chlorobenzene is required then chlorine needs to be bubbled through benzene 'in the dark' with iron(III) chloride, $FeCl_3$, or aluminium chloride, $AlCl_3$, often used as the catalyst.

The alkylation of benzene

This reaction is often called the Friedel-Crafts reaction, after the scientists who discovered it. The term 'alkylation' means the substitution of an alkyl group such as methyl, $-CH_3$, or ethyl, $-CH_2CH_3$. This reaction is carried out in a similar way to the halogenation of benzene but, for example, chloromethane is used in place of bromine. Again, a catalyst is used – the commonest one is aluminium chloride:

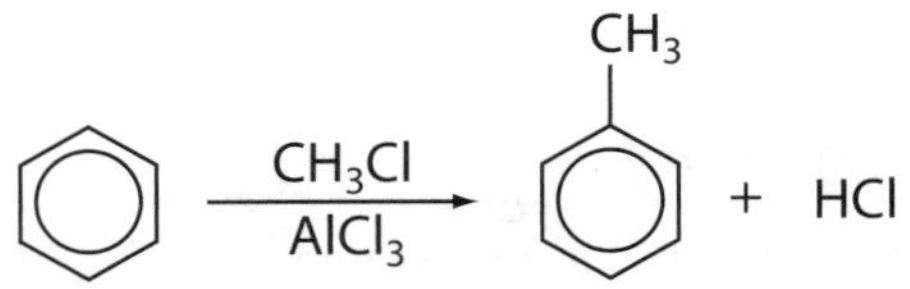

The mechanism is again electrophilic substitution and is similar to those given above:

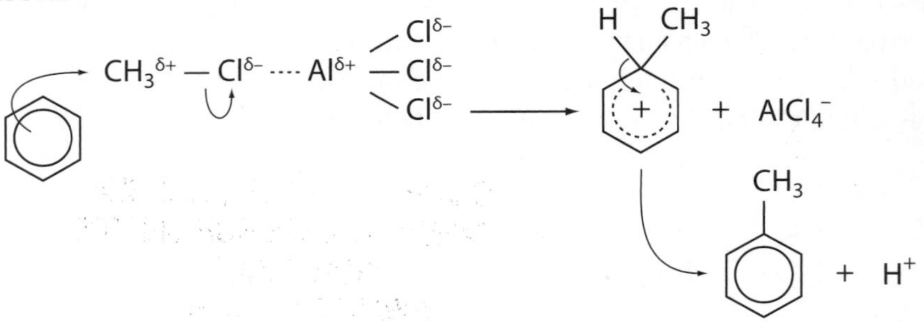

The alkaline hydrolysis of chloroalkanes and chlorobenzene

A chloroalkane, such as 1-chlorobutane, reacts easily with sodium hydroxide solution when the mixture is refluxed, giving butan-1-ol as the organic product:

$$CH_3CH_2CH_2CH_2Cl + NaOH \rightarrow CH_3CH_2CH_2CH_2OH + NaCl$$

In the CH2 unit you are required to know that the mechanism of this reaction is nucleophilic substitution:

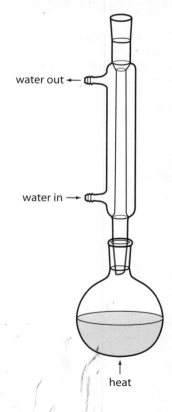

However benzene, with its stable π-ring system of electrons is not very likely to react with a nucleophile. The previous pages have reminded you that benzene tends to react mainly with electrophiles. In chlorobenzene the bond between the chlorine atom and the carbon atom is stronger than the aliphatic C—Cl bond found in 1-chlorobutane.

Bond	Bond energy kJ mol^{-1}
Aliphatic C—Cl	346
Aromatic C—Cl	399

This stronger bond between carbon and chlorine in chlorobenzene results from the non-bonding lone pairs overlapping with the ring π-system of electrons. The resulting bond needs much more energy to be broken. It is possible to make phenol from chlorobenzene but forcing conditions of temperature and pressure are required, not just simple refluxing at around 100°C.

As a result, phenol cannot be made from chlorobenzene except under extreme conditions, which are not economically viable. In industry phenol is generally made from 2-propylbenzene (cumene). This has the advantage that propanone is a co-product of the reaction.

Key Term

Bond energy = the energy needed to break a covalent bond into its constituent 'atoms' (in the gas phase). The higher the value then the stronger the bond.

Grade boost

A weak area for many candidates in the examination is the description of practical work. Candidates may be asked to describe what is meant by 'refluxing'.

Your response should state that evaporation and condensation are occurring and that the condensed material returns to the flask where the reaction is going on. If you do not say 'returns' to the flask, then you could be describing distillation!

Organic compounds containing oxygen

Forming primary and secondary alcohols

There are two main methods of forming primary and secondary alcohols:

- Substitution of the halogen atom in a halogenoalkane by a hydroxyl group
- Reduction of an aldehyde or ketone.

From a halogenoalkane

This is a nucleophilic substitution reaction and is carried out by refluxing together the halogenoalkane and aqueous sodium (or potassium) hydroxide. Equations can be written using chemical formulae or as an ionic equation:

$$CH_3CH_2CH_2Br + NaOH \rightarrow CH_3CH_2CH_2OH + NaBr$$
1-bromopropane   propan-1-ol

$$ClCH_2CH_2CH_2CH_2Cl + 2OH^- \rightarrow HOCH_2CH_2CH_2CH_2OH + 2Cl^-$$
1,4-dichlorobutane   butane-1,4-diol

The mechanism for this reaction is mentioned in the CH2 specification but you could be asked to give it in this unit too!

It is important to remember that halogen atoms bonded directly to benzene rings cannot readily react in this way. For example, it is very difficult to produce phenol from chlorobenzene by this method.

From an aldehyde or ketone

This is a reduction reaction that is carried out by reacting together the aldehyde or ketone and the reducing agent sodium tetrahydridoborate(III), $NaBH_4$, dissolved in water. This compound has the common name 'sodium borohydride'. It is quite acceptable for you to represent this reducing agent as [H] in the equation. An alternative reducing agent could be lithium tetrahydridoaluminate (III), $LiAlH_4$ (or lithium aluminium hydride), dissolved in a suitable solvent such as ethoxyethane, but this is a much more hazardous process!

$$CH_3CH_2COCH_3 + 2[H] \rightarrow CH_3CH_2CH(OH)CH_3$$
butanone   butan-2-ol

$$CH_3CH_2CH_2CH_2CHO + 2[H] \rightarrow CH_3CH_2CH_2CH_2CH_2OH$$
pentanal   pentan-1-ol

The production of esters and alkenes from alcohols

Key Term

Esters = contain the −C(O)O− group bonded to alkyl or aryl groups.

Esters are often sweet smelling liquids and there is much interest in their production and uses as solvents and in perfumery. There are two methods that are needed for this specification.

From an alcohol and an acid chloride

Primary and secondary alcohols react with an acid chloride, such as ethanoyl chloride to give an ester and the co-product hydrogen chloride:

$$CH_3-C\overset{O}{\underset{Cl}{<}} + CH_3CH_2OH \longrightarrow CH_3-C\overset{O}{\underset{OCH_2CH_3}{<}} + HCl$$

ethanoyl chloride   ethanol   ethyl ethanoate

You should note that this method gives off the irritating gas hydrogen chloride and is a method that needs to be done in the fume cupboard. As a result the method that uses a carboxylic acid is often preferred.

> **Grade boost**
>
> An alcohol such as butan-2-ol is a useful compound for examiners to ask about. In questions on dehydration there are two alkenes that could be produced.
>
> These are but-1-ene and but-2-ene. Of course there are really three, since but-2-ene can exist as *E*- and *Z*-isomers.

From an alcohol and a carboxylic acid

An ester can also be produced by reacting together a primary or secondary alcohol and a carboxylic acid. A little concentrated sulfuric acid is generally used as a catalyst. The reaction mixture is refluxed – often using a water bath or using an electrical heater because of the dangers of fire from direct heating. Any remaining acid is then neutralised using sodium hydrogencarbonate solution in a separating funnel. (After removal of water, the mixture is distilled and the ester collected at its boiling temperature.)

$$CH_3CH_2C\overset{O}{\underset{OH}{<}} + CH_3\underset{OH}{CHCH_3} \longrightarrow CH_3CH_2C\overset{O}{<}\underset{O-C-H}{\overset{CH_3}{<}}\underset{CH_3}{} + H_2O$$

propanoic acid   propan-2-ol   2-propyl propanoate

Dehydration of alcohols

An alkene results when alcohols are dehydrated. This process of removal of water can be done in a number of ways. The alcohol can be warmed and its vapour passed over aluminium oxide or pieces of broken pot. In the laboratory the traditional method is to warm the alcohol with an excess of concentrated sulfuric or phosphoric acids.

cyclohexanol   cyclohexene

> **Pointer**
>
> The equation given shows the dehydration of cyclohexanol. This is a common reaction in the laboratory because both the secondary alcohol cyclohexanol and the product cyclohexene are liquids with boiling temperatures that are suitable for normal laboratory conditions.

Sometimes candidates choose to give the formula of the oxidising agent rather than its name. This is generally acceptable but the formula must be correct. For example, CrO_7^{2-} is wrong, as is MnO_4^{2-}.

It is also wrong to omit 'acidified' or H^+.

If potassium manganate(VII) has been chosen, then it must have its correct oxidation state to gain any credit.

If you are using potassium manganate(VII) then 'colourless' is correct but 'clear' is definitely wrong!

Pointer

Any aldehydes or ketones present as a result of oxidation will give an orange-red solid with 2,4-dinitrophenylhydrazine.

Pointer

Ethanol as a biofuel

There is an increasing interest in fuels that are obtained from renewable sources. Ethanol has been used in this way for a number of years, especially in South America. Sugar cane residues, for example, can be fermented to give ethanol and then mixed with petrol or, increasingly, as a fuel in its own right.

The oxidation of primary and secondary alcohols

The oxidation (shown as [O] below) of these alcohols is an essential part of any revision and is a near certainty for an examination question. Important sequences to remember are:

'Oxidation' here means the removal of 'hydrogen' or the addition of 'oxygen'. If a balanced equation is required, then [O] can be used as the formula for the oxidising agent, rather than its chemical formula:

propan-1-ol → propanal

and then

propanal → propanoic acid

You will not need to balance an equation using the formula of the actual oxidising agent but you will be expected to know what is being used. The most common oxidising agent is 'acidified dichromate solution'. This generally means potassium dichromate ($K_2Cr_2O_7$) dissolved in strong aqueous sulfuric acid (H_2SO_4). The colour change that you should know is orange to green as the orange dichromate is reduced to green chromium(III) ions, Cr^{3+}(aq). If the aldehyde is required, then it is distilled off as it is formed, otherwise it tends to be further oxidised to the carboxylic acid. Potassium manganate(VII) (permanganate) and aqueous sulfuric acid can also be used as the oxidising agent. The colour change for this is purple to colourless, as the manganate(VII) ions are reduced to aqueous Mn^{2+} ions. The presence of an aldehyde in the product can be detected using 2,4-dinitrophenylhydrazine, and any carboxylic acid present will 'fizz' if a carbonate is added. A secondary alcohol will be oxidised to a ketone and no further oxidation will occur under these conditions.

The reactions of phenol

Phenols are benzene ring compounds with a hydroxyl group bonded **directly** to the ring:

phenol   2,4-dichlorophenol   1,2-dihydroxybenzene

The presence of the benzene ring tends to weaken the O−H bond. This means that phenols are acidic in aqueous solution, tending to lose protons:

phenoxide ion

The phenoxide ion is more stable than expected because the negative charge tends to be spread out 'around' the ring.

One test for phenols is their reaction with neutral iron(III) chloride solution, $FeCl_3(aq)$. These react together to give a purple solution containing a soluble complex. This purple colour is not given by alcohols and is a distinguishing test between phenols and alcohols.

Phenol will react with an acid chloride to give an ester. An alcohol will react similarly:

phenyl ethanoate

The presence of the −OH group bonded directly to the benzene ring increases the electron density of the ring. This makes phenol more susceptible to electrophilic substitution. As a result, phenol is a much more reactive compound than benzene. Unfortunately the electron density of the ring is not the same at the five remaining positions. The electron density is particularly increased at the 2-, 4- and 6- positions. Aqueous bromine (bromine water) will react with phenol to give a white precipitate of 2, 4, 6-tribromophenol:

$+ 3 Br_2 \longrightarrow$ $+ 3 HBr$

quickfire

⑮ The formula for 2-methylphenol is drawn below:

Draw the structure of an isomer of 2-methylphenol that will not give a purple coloured solution when it is reacted with iron(III) chloride solution.

≫ Pointer

This reaction between phenol and bromine results in the decolourisation of the 'orange' aqueous bromine. It is important to note that alkenes also decolourise aqueous bromine but they do not give a white precipitate.

Ketones = fit the formula R – C(O) – R' , where R and R' are alkyl or aryl groups.

 Pointer

The reactions of ketones are usually given by aldehydes. However, aldehydes have 'extra' reactions because they have a hydrogen atom directly bonded to the carbon atom of the carbonyl group.

quickfire

⑯ Here are the names of five compounds:

- ethanedioic acid
- hex-2-ene
- propane-1,2-diol
- butanone
- methanal.

Select which of these compounds will:

a) decolourise aqueous bromine

b) give a silver mirror with Tollens' reagent

c) react with acidified dichromate but **not** give a silver mirror with Tollens' reagent

d) not give a red/brown solid with Fehling's reagent but will give an orange solid with 2,4-DNP.

Identifying aldehydes and ketones

You will remember that aldehydes and **ketones** are carbonyl compounds (they contain the C=O group) and that the difference between them is that aldehydes contain at least one hydrogen atom bonded to the carbon atom of the carbonyl group. Ketones do not have this hydrogen and the carbon atom of the carbonyl group is bonded directly to two other carbon atoms.

$$CH_3CH_2CH_2 \diagdown \atop H \diagup C=O \qquad CH_3CH_2 \diagdown \atop CH_3 \diagup C=O$$

butanal   butanone

This hydrogen atom of the aldehyde group is quite reactive and one result is that aldehydes can be easily oxidised to carboxylic acids. As they are being oxidised, this means that they are themselves acting as reducing agents. Ketones are unable to react in this way as they do not contain this reactive hydrogen atom directly bonded to the carbon atom of a carbonyl group. There are two tests that rely on the reducing ability of an aldehyde and these are used to distinguish an aldehyde from a ketone.

Tollens' reagent

This reagent is made, when required, by adding aqueous ammonia to an aqueous solution of silver nitrate until the brown precipitate that is formed just dissolves to give a colourless solution. An alternative name for Tollens' reagent is ammoniacal silver nitrate solution. A little of the suspected aldehyde is added to some Tollens' reagent in a test tube and the tube put into a beaker of warm water. A silver mirror is slowly formed on the inside of the tube. The aldehyde has acted as a reducing agent and reduced aqueous silver ions to silver metal that then 'plates' the inside of the test tube.

$$Ag^+(aq) \ + \ e^- \ \rightarrow \ Ag(s)$$

Fehling's reagent

This is a dark blue solution that contains complexed Cu^{2+} ions. It is made by mixing a copper(II) containing solution with sodium hydroxide solution. Benedict's reagent is a similar copper containing reagent that reacts in the same way as Fehling's reagent. The result of these tests with reducing agents gives a red-brown precipitate of copper(I) oxide, Cu_2O, as copper(II) ions are reduced to the copper(I) state. A simple equation showing this reduction could be:

$$2Cu^{2+}(aq) \ + \ 2OH^-(aq) \ + \ 2e^- \ \rightarrow \ Cu_2O(s) \ + \ H_2O(l)$$

This test for an aldehyde is carried out in a similar way to the Tollens' test.

Acidified dichromate

As we have seen on a previous page, an aldehyde (but not a ketone) will reduce 'acidified dichromate' solution from **orange** to **green** as Cr^{3+} ions are formed. If you use this as a test then it is essential to have an excess of the aldehyde, otherwise some orange will remain and 'spoil' any colour change that may occur.

Tests for aldehydes and ketones that are given by both types of compounds

The tests with both Tollens' and Fehling's reagents are positive for an aldehyde and **not** a ketone because of the presence of an 'oxidisable' hydrogen atom in an aldehyde.

Any test that is positive for just the carbonyl group will be given by both aldehydes and ketones. The only test that you are required to know is the test that uses a solution of 2,4-dinitrophenylhydrazine (shortened to 2,4-DNP or Brady's reagent). It is not necessary to know the formula of 2,4-DNP or the formula of the product obtained when an aldehyde or ketone reacts with it. However, you do need to know that the reaction is nucleophilic addition followed by the elimination of a small molecule (water). This is often shortened to nucleophilic addition – elimination and sometimes also simply described as a condensation reaction. The aldehyde or ketone will react with 2,4-dinitrophenylhydrazine to give a distinctive orange-red precipitate. This is filtered off and purified. The melting temperature of the solid is then taken and compared with text book values of melting temperatures. The value will then identify the starting aldehyde or ketone. Many aldehydes and ketones are liquids of fairly low boiling point and their flammable nature often makes it difficult to identify them simply, safely and accurately just from their boiling temperature. The melting temperature range of the 2,4-DNP derivative is suitable for most melting temperature determinations, perhaps 75°C to about 175°C. An example of this is ethanal.

Ethanal boils at 21°C but its 2,4-DNP derivative melts at 147°C.

Tests for the $CH_3C=O$ group in ketones

Compounds that contain the $CH_3C=O$ group include propanone and butanone. When these are reacted with an alkaline solution of iodine (or an aqueous mixture of sodium chlorate(I) and potassium iodide) a yellow precipitate of triiodomethane (iodoform), CHI_3, is formed. A positive result to this test is also given by compounds that contain the $CH_3CH(OH)$ group, as this is oxidised to the $CH_3C=O$ group during the reaction. This means that ethanol and propan-2-ol also react in this way but not propan-1-ol.

Grade boost

The test for the $CH_3C=O$ group in ketones is sometimes called the 'iodoform' reaction. Do not use iodoform (triiodomethane) as one of the reactants. It is the product in a positive test!

Pointer

Aldehydes will also react with acidified manganate(VII) solution, as they are oxidised to carboxylic acids. The colour change is from purple to colourless for the manganese compounds. Ketones will not react.

The addition of hydrogen cyanide to carbonyl compounds

Carbonyl compounds are those compounds that contain a carbonyl (C=O) group. Of course this can mean, in addition to aldehydes and ketones, carboxylic acids, esters, acid chlorides and amides. Fortunately, we only need to know about the reaction of hydrogen cyanide with aldehydes and ketones. Using old-fashioned terms this reaction forms a way of 'ascending the **homologous series**'. This really means creating a new carbon to carbon bond so that the carbon chain length is increased. It can also lead to the introduction of new functional groups into the molecule – a useful method for proceeding further.

A typical reaction is the reaction of hydrogen cyanide with ethanal:

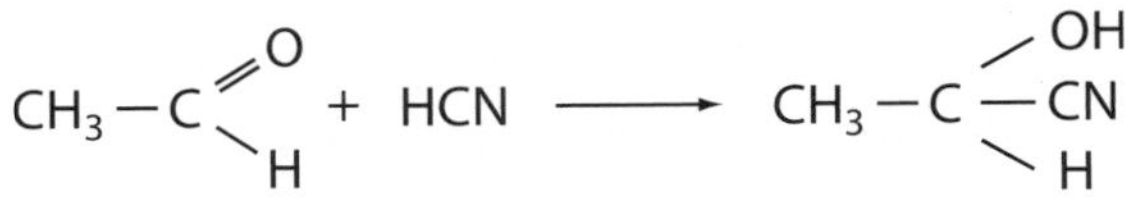

The product is 2-hydroxypropanenitrile and as such, is not a particularly useful material. However, hydrolysis of the nitrile group, often carried out by warming with dilute sulfuric acid, is 2-hydroxypropanoic acid (or lactic acid). This can be converted to other compounds:

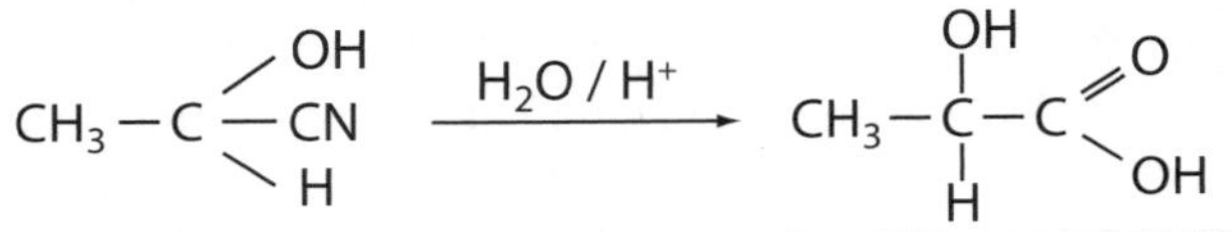

The mechanism of the reaction

Aldehydes and ketones contain a polar carbonyl group, $C^{\delta+}=O^{\delta-}$. This allows them to be attacked by nucleophiles or electrophiles. Although hydrogen cyanide is a weak acid, there are some free cyanide ions to attack the ethanal. The first stage in the mechanism is the attack of a cyanide ion (the nucleophile) on the $\delta+$ carbon atom of the carbonyl group. Increased polarisation of the carbonyl group then allows a hydrogen ion from the hydrogen cyanide to bond with the resulting negatively charged oxygen atom giving an alcohol group. This mechanism is called nucleophilic addition because the CN^- nucleophile initially attacks the $\delta+$ carbon atom and the hydrogen ion is then attached to the oxygen 'atom'. Addition of HCN has effectively occurred across the carbon to oxygen double bond.

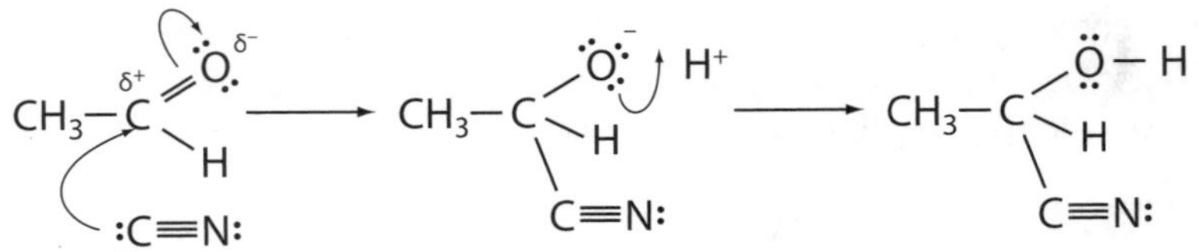

Ketones react in a similar way, for example propanone gives 2-hydroxy-2-methylpropanenitrile, $CH_3C(OH)(CH_3)CN$.

Key Term

Homologous series = a family of compounds that have the same general formula and contain the same functional group.

Pointer

This is a very important section for examiners, as they can ask about the mechanism and then ask further questions about the hydroxynitrile and compounds formed from it.

Grade boost

If the question starts with ethanal, you will end up with 2-hydroxypropanoic acid after hydrolysis of the product. The examiner could then ask about this acid as it contains a chiral centre and is both an acid and an alcohol!

quickfire

⑰ The formula of the product formed by the nucleophilic addition of hydrogen cyanide to an aldehyde or ketone is $CH_3CH_2C(OH)(CH_2CH_3)CN$.

Give the name of the starting aldehyde or ketone.

Physical properties of carboxylic acids

Carboxylic acids are compounds with the functional group –COOH. The lower members are colourless liquids with a 'sharp' smell. Vinegar is a dilute aqueous solution of ethanoic acid. Some properties of carboxylic acids are shown in the table.

Carboxylic acid	Formula	Boiling temp. °C	Solubility in water
methanoic	H-COOH	101	soluble
ethanoic	CH_3–COOH	118	soluble
propanoic	CH_3CH_2–COOH	141	soluble
hexanoic	$CH_3(CH_2)_4$–COOH	205	insoluble

You will notice that boiling temperatures rise as the length of the carbon chain increases. This is because of increasing van der Waals forces between the molecules, meaning that more energy is needed to overcome these forces, resulting in a higher boiling temperature. Those carboxylic acids that are soluble in water hydrogen bond with water molecules. The polar atoms of the hydroxyl group are attracted to polar atoms of the water molecule:

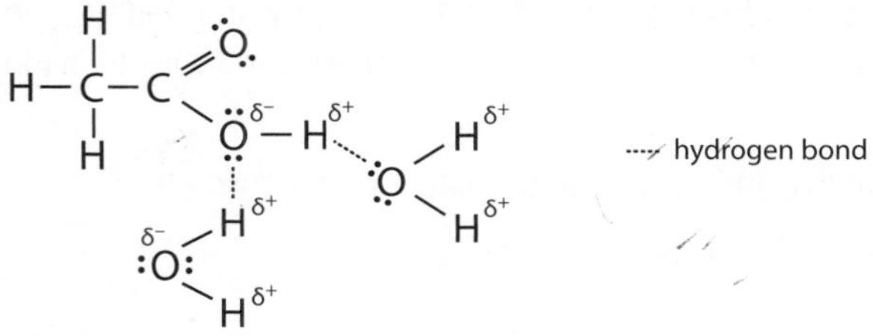

As the carbon chain length increases, the acids become less water soluble. This is because the polar acid (COOH) group is becoming a smaller part of the whole molecule. The alkyl group has little attraction for the water molecules. The presence of the acid group means that there are stronger forces between the acid molecules, as hydrogen bonding can occur between these molecules:

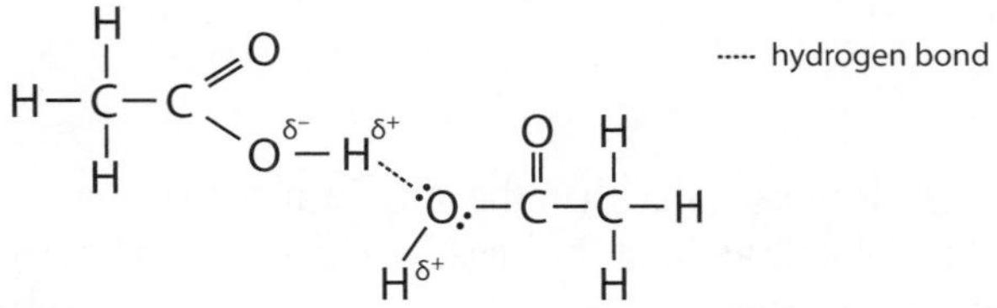

As a result a carboxylic acid will have a much higher boiling temperature than the equivalent alkane, where the forces between molecules are much weaker. This is shown in the table where the boiling temperatures of pentane and pentanoic acid are compared.

Compound	Formula	Boiling temp. °C
pentane	$CH_3(CH_2)_3CH_3$	36
pentanoic acid	$CH_3(CH_2)_3COOH$	186

quickfire

(18) Use the table to predict the boiling temperature of butanoic acid, $CH_3(CH_2)_2COOH$.

Give a reason for your answer.

quickfire

(19) Butanedioic acid, $HOOC(CH_2)_2COOH$, is a solid that is quite soluble in water.

Briefly explain these two facts.

» Pointer

Hydrogen bonding is a weak form of bonding that occurs between a hydrogen atom (bonded to nitrogen, oxygen or fluorine) and a nitrogen, oxygen or fluorine atom of another molecule.

An acid = a compound that is a proton donor (H^+). Most carboxylic acids and phenols are weak acids, as they only partially dissociate into ions in aqueous solution.

The relative acidities of carboxylic acids, phenol, alcohols and water

A compound can act as **an acid** if it produces hydrogen ions, $H^+(aq)$, when it 'dissolves' in water, for example:

$$CH_3COOH(aq) + H_2O(l) \rightarrow CH_3COO^- + H_3O^+(aq)$$

The equation shows the hydrogen ion as its hydrated form, $H_3O^+(aq)$ but we often use $H^+(aq)$, for simplicity. The extent to which hydrogen ions are formed gives a measure of acidity. In the CH5 unit you study K_a, which is a measure of the extent to which this dissociation into ions has occurred. In simple terms we can look at the pH of aqueous solutions (of the same concentration) to compare acid strengths of various types of compounds. An example of this is shown in the table.

compound	pH
ethanoic acid	2.9
phenol	5.5
water	7.0
ethanol	~7.5

You will see that ethanoic acid is the strongest acid and that water and ethanol are not really acidic at all. So what are the reasons for these variations in acidity?

Ethanoic acid

When added to water, hydrogen ions and ethanoate ions are formed:

$$CH_3COOH_{(aq)} \rightleftharpoons CH_3COO^-_{(aq)} + H^+_{(aq)}$$

The extent to which hydrogen ions are formed depends partly on the stability of the starting materials and products. The ethanoate ion (and similar ions formed from other carboxylic acids) are more stable than the ions formed from ethanol and water, because the negative charge can be delocalised across several atoms.

$$\left[CH_3-C\underset{\diagdown O}{\overset{\diagup O}{}} \right]^-$$

Phenol

The phenoxide ion, $C_6H_5O^-$, is more stable than the ions formed by water and ethanol because of the delocalisation of the negative charge around the π-electron ring system of the benzene.

Ethanol

There is little tendency for ethanol molecules to ionise as the ethoxide ion, $C_2H_5O^-$, is not stabilised by delocalisation.

Both phenol and ethanoic acid can be neutralised by an alkali such as sodium hydroxide, giving a salt. However, only a carboxylic acid is sufficiently acidic to produce carbon dioxide when a carbonate is added. This test provides a way of showing the difference in the relative acidities of these compounds.

» *Pointer*

The equation for the neutralisation of phenol by sodium hydroxide is

$C_6H_5OH + NaOH$
$\rightarrow C_6H_5O^-Na^+ + H_2O$

Grade boost

Make sure that if the question asks for observations – you give them!

For example, 'fizzing' is an observation but 'carbon dioxide is produced' is not.

Forming carboxylic acids by oxidation

The oxidation of primary alcohols and aldehydes

Primary alcohols (but not secondary alcohols) can be oxidised to carboxylic acids using a suitable oxidising agent. In the following equation the oxidising agent is represented by [O]:

$$R-\underset{\underset{H}{|}}{\overset{\overset{H}{|}}{C}}-OH \xrightarrow{[O]} R-C\underset{H}{\overset{O}{\diagup}} \xrightarrow{[O]} R-C\underset{OH}{\overset{O}{\diagup}}$$

The usual oxidising agent is acidified potassium dichromate solution – a solution of potassium dichromate in strong aqueous sulfuric acid. This is sometimes represented by the 'formula' $H^+(aq)/Cr_2O_7^{2-}(aq)$. To produce the carboxylic acid, the alcohol or aldehyde is refluxed with an excess of the oxidising agent The colour change is from orange to green as dichromate ions, $Cr_2O_7^{2-}$, are reduced to green chromium(III), $Cr^{3+}(aq)$ ions, but of course an excess of the orange dichromate is present!

Alternatively, a strong oxidising agent, such as acidified potassium manganate(VII) solution, can be used. This solution of potassium manganate(VII) in strong aqueous sulfuric acid can be represented as the 'formula' $H^+(aq)/MnO_4^-(aq)$. This mixture is refluxed with the alcohol or aldehyde. The purple manganate(VII) ions are reduced to 'colourless' $Mn^{2+}(aq)$ ions. This colour change may be difficult to notice as an excess of the manganate(VII) is used. In either preparation the carboxylic acid is distilled from the reaction mixture and purified.

The oxidation of alkylbenzenes

Aromatic carboxylic acids, such as benzenecarboxylic acid (benzoic acid), C_6H_5COOH, can be obtained by refluxing together an alkylbenzene with alkaline potassium manganate(VII) solution. An alkylbenzene is a benzene hydrocarbon with, e.g., a methyl group substituted in place of a hydrogen atom. An overall equation is:

$$CH_3-\text{(benzene ring)} \xrightarrow{3\,[O]} COOH-\text{(benzene ring)} + 2H_2O$$

> **Grade boost**
>
> When oxidising an alkylbenzene with alkaline manganate(VII) solution, do not forget to acidify the product to obtain the carboxylic acid.

The purple solution of potassium manganate(VII) is reduced to brown manganese(IV) oxide, seen as a brown sludge. Since this reaction takes place in an alkaline solution the organic product is, e.g., sodium benzenecarboxylate (sodium benzoate), $C_6H_5COO^-Na^+$. The mixture is then acidified with a dilute acid (e.g., HCl(aq)) when white crystals of benzenecarboxylic acid are produced.

Key terms

Decarboxylation = the loss of a carboxyl group (literally CO_2). A decarboxylation reaction leads to a reduction in the length of the carbon chain.

≫ Pointer

In general, decarboxylation reactions give poor yields. Although we can write a simple equation for the reaction (and this is all that is required for the examination), many other reactions are also occurring. Bond fission occurs at several places in the carbon chain, giving a variety of products.

◉⟪ quickfire

 20 State the name of the alkane obtained if sodium hexanoate is strongly heated with sodalime.

⩓ Grade boost

Candidates often have trouble in clearly giving the name of the reducing agent whose formula is $LiAlH_4$. Although examiners have tended to be lenient with such a tricky name – do try and learn that it is lithium tetrahydridoaluminate(III).

The reduction of carboxylic acids

Carboxylic acids are stable compounds and a powerful reducing agent is needed to reverse the oxidation process that gave them and to produce aldehydes and primary alcohols. The reducing agent that is used is lithium tetrahydridoaluminate(III), $LiAlH_4$. This compound reacts violently with water and so it is dissolved in a non-aqueous solvent (usually ethoxyethane). A chemical equation is required for this reaction but the reducing agent can be represented by [H]:

$$CH_3-C\overset{O}{\underset{OH}{\diagup}} \xrightarrow{4\,[H]} CH_3-C\overset{OH}{\underset{H}{-H}} + H_2O$$

When a carboxylic acid (or more usually its sodium salt) is strongly heated with an alkali such as solid sodium hydroxide or sodalime, decarboxylation occurs and an alkane is produced, together with a carbonate. An example is the **decarboxylation** of sodium propanoate. Sodalime is a mixture prepared by heating together sodium hydroxide and calcium oxide. However, for simplicity, in equations we represent its formula as NaOH:

$$CH_3CH_2COO^-Na^+(s) + NaOH(s) \rightarrow \underset{\text{ethane}}{C_2H_6(g)} + Na_2CO_3(s)$$

If the salt of an aromatic acid is used then an aromatic hydrocarbon is the organic product:

$$\underset{\substack{\text{sodium}\\\text{benzenecarboxylate}}}{C_6H_5COO^-Na^+(s)} + NaOH(s) \rightarrow \underset{\text{benzene}}{C_6H_6(g)} + Na_2CO_3(s)$$

This reaction is an example of 'descending the homologous series' – this phrase means a reaction that reduces the length of the carbon chain.

If the calcium salt of the carboxylic acid is strongly heated then decarboxylation also occurs and the product is an aldehyde or ketone. For example, the decarboxylation of calcium ethanoate gives propanone:

$$(CH_3COO)_2Ca \rightarrow CH_3COCH_3 + CaCO_3$$

Forming acid chlorides from carboxylic acids and their reactions

An acid chloride is a compound of general formula CH_3COCl. They differ from the formula of a carboxylic acid in that the $-OH$ group of the acid has been replaced by a chlorine atom.

Making acid chlorides

There are three common ways to produce these compounds from carboxylic acids. The usual method (given in books!) is to react the acid with phosphorus(V) chloride (phosphorus pentachloride), PCl_5. Other routes use the acid and phosphorus(III) chloride (phosphorus trichloride), PCl_3, or the carboxylic acid and sulfur dichloride oxide (thionyl chloride), $SOCl_2$. Two typical equations are given below:

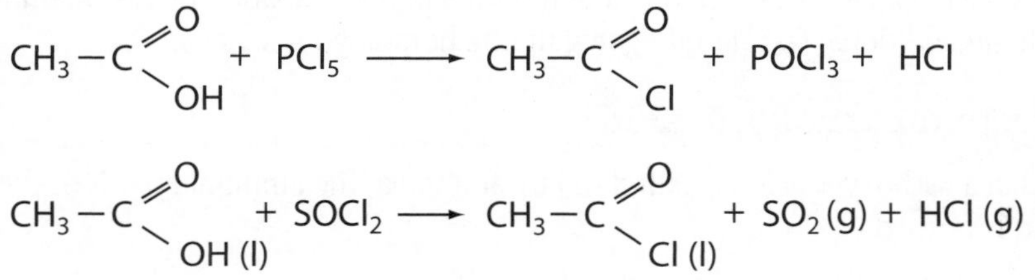

$$CH_3-C{\overset{O}{\underset{OH}{}}} + PCl_5 \longrightarrow CH_3-C{\overset{O}{\underset{Cl}{}}} + POCl_3 + HCl$$

$$CH_3-C{\overset{O}{\underset{OH\ (l)}{}}} + SOCl_2 \longrightarrow CH_3-C{\overset{O}{\underset{Cl\ (l)}{}}} + SO_2\,(g) + HCl\,(g)$$

The second method (using sulfur dichloride oxide) has the advantage that two of the products are gaseous and easily lost from the reaction mixture. The remaining product, the wanted material, is a liquid and can easily be purified by distillation.

Reactions of acid chlorides

Acid chlorides are useful compounds as they are very reactive.

- They react with alcohols giving esters:

$$CH_3COCl + CH_3OH \rightarrow CH_3COOCH_3 + HCl$$
methyl ethanoate

- They also react violently with water, giving the parent carboxylic acid:

$$CH_3COCl + H_2O \rightarrow CH_3COOH + HCl$$
ethanoic acid

- They react with salts of carboxylic acids to produce acid anhydrides of which an example is ethanoic anhydride (acetic anhydride), $(CH_3CO)_2O$:

Acid anhydrides are also very useful and reactive compounds. They have the advantage that they are not as violently reactive as acid chlorides! Ethanoic anhydride is used to make cellulose-based polymers and in the production of aspirin.

⊙ ⊀⊀⊀⊀ **quicKpire**

㉑ State the name of the compound that has the formula:

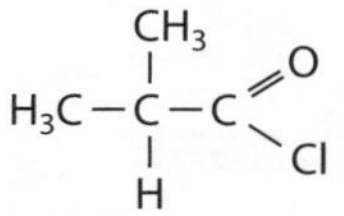

$$H_3C-\underset{\underset{H}{|}}{\overset{\overset{CH_3}{|}}{C}}-C{\overset{O}{\underset{Cl}{}}}$$

⊙ ⊀⊀⊀⊀ **quicKpire**

㉒ Two moles of ethanoic acid react with PCl_5 to give an 80% yield of ethanoyl chloride. Calculate the mass of ethanoyl chloride that is obtained.

[M_r of ethanoyl chloride is 78.5]

» *Pointer*

One disadvantage of using ethanoic anhydride rather than ethanoyl chloride in a reaction is that ethanoic acid is a co-product. This may be difficult to separate from the required product.

Key Term

Hydrolysis = decomposition by the addition of water, usually irreversibly. The added water may be in the form of water itself, aqueous acid or alkali.

Grade boost

Nitriles can be tricky to name. It is important to remember that the carbon of the cyanide group is included as part of the longest carbon chain when you name the compound.

quickfire

㉓ Name the nitrile that has the formula:

$CH_3CH(CH_3)CH_2CN$

quickfire

㉔ You are given a sample of bromomethane. Your task is to produce ethylamine from it in just two stages. State the reagents and any essential conditions for each stage.

Organic compounds containing nitrogen

Making and reacting nitriles

Nitriles are organic compounds of nitrogen, they contain the cyanide group, −CN. There are two common methods of forming these compounds.

From a halogenoalkane

Nitriles are formed by the reaction of a halogenoalkane and potassium cyanide, using ethanol as the solvent:

$$CH_3CH_2CH_2Br \ + \ KCN \ \longrightarrow \ CH_3CH_2CH_2CN \ + \ KBr$$
1-bromopropane   butanenitrile

This nucleophilic substitution reaction results in the formation of a compound with an additional C–C bond ('going up the homologous series').

From a carboxylic acid

When a carboxylic acid is neutralised by ammonia, the ammonium salt of the acid is formed:

$$CH_3COOH \ + \ NH_3 \ \rightarrow \ CH_3COONH_4^+$$
                                    ammonium ethanoate

If the ammonium salt is then heated, water is lost and an amide is formed:

$$CH_3{-}COO^-NH_4^+ \xrightarrow{\ -H_2O\ } CH_3{-}C\overset{\displaystyle O}{\underset{\displaystyle NH_2}{}}$$

The amide can be strongly heated with a dehydrating agent (such as phosphorus(V) oxide, P_4O_{10}) when more water is lost, giving a nitrile:

$$CH_3{-}C\overset{\displaystyle O}{\underset{\displaystyle NH_2}{}} \xrightarrow{\ -H_2O\ } CH_3{-}C{\equiv}N$$

Hydrolysis of nitriles and amides

If a nitrile or amide is warmed with dilute sulfuric acid, **hydrolysis** occurs giving the carboxylic acid:

$$CH_3{-}C{\equiv}N \xrightarrow{\ H^+/H_2O\ } CH_3{-}C\overset{\displaystyle O}{\underset{\displaystyle NH_2}{}} \xrightarrow{\ H^+/H_2O\ } CH_3{-}C\overset{\displaystyle O}{\underset{\displaystyle OH}{}}$$

The reduction of a nitrile

A nitrile is reduced by lithium tetrahydridoaluminate(III) (dissolved in ethoxyethane) producing an amine. This is an example of an addition reaction, as hydrogen is added across the carbon to nitrogen triple bond:

$$CH_3{-}C{\equiv}N \xrightarrow{\ 4[H]\ } CH_3{-}CH_2{-}NH_2$$

Making and reacting aliphatic and aromatic amines

Aliphatic amines can be made by a substitution reaction from a halogenoalkane, whereas aromatic amines cannot be made this way in the laboratory, but are made by the reduction of nitrobenzenes.

Making aliphatic amines

This is another example of nucleophilic substitution and these amines are made by reacting a halogenoalkane with an excess of ammonia, dissolved in ethanol. A hydrogen halide is also produced and this reacts with excess ammonia, giving an ammonium salt:

$$CH_3CH_2CH_2CH_2Br + 2NH_3 \rightarrow CH_3CH_2CH_2CH_2NH_2 + NH_4Br$$

1-bromobutane   butylamine

Making aromatic amines

A nitro compound is heated with an appropriate reducing agent, such as tin and concentrated hydrochloric acid (shown as [H] in the equation):

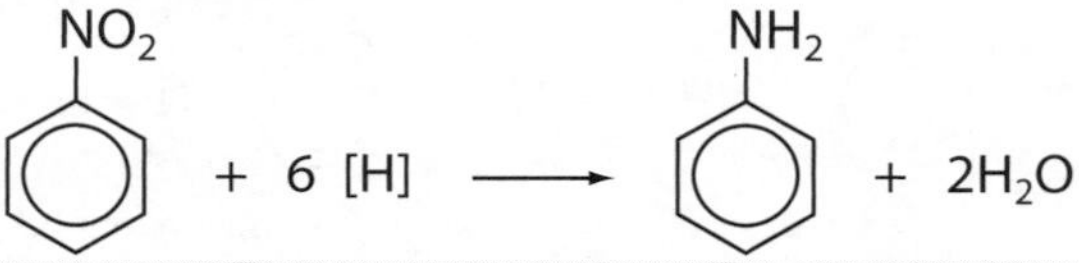

The basicity of amines

The nitrogen atom in the amine group has a lone pair of electrons. These can act as a base by forming a co-ordinate bond with a hydrogen ion:

$$CH_3NH_2 + HCl \rightarrow CH_3NH_3^+Cl^-$$

As a result an aqueous solution of an amine has a pH of greater than 7 and turns Universal Indicator to a blue colour. Only 'smaller' amines are soluble in water but 'all' amines react as bases by being electron pair donors/proton acceptors.

Ethanoylation of amines

The hydrogen atom of the amine group can be substituted by an ethanoyl group, $CH_3C=O$, giving a substituted amine:

$$C_6H_5NH_2 + CH_3COCl \longrightarrow C_6H_5NHCOCH_3 + HCl$$

Key Term

Primary amine = an organic compound where a carbon atom in an open chain or ring is bonded to an $-NH_2$ group.

Grade boost

The chemistry of amines is often taught late in the second year of the specification. This is a popular topic for examiners' questions but it seems that questions on this topic are often answered poorly by many candidates. Make sure that you know all about aliphatic and aromatic amines!

quickfire

㉕ Name the aliphatic amine that reacts with an excess of hydrochloric acid to give a compound of formula:

$$CH_3(CH_2)_4NH_3^+Cl^-$$

quickfire

㉖ 1,6-diaminohexane can be used to make polyamides. Give the structural formula of the halogenoalkane that will react with ammonia to give 1,6-diaminohexane.

The reaction of amines with nitric(III) acid (nitrous acid)

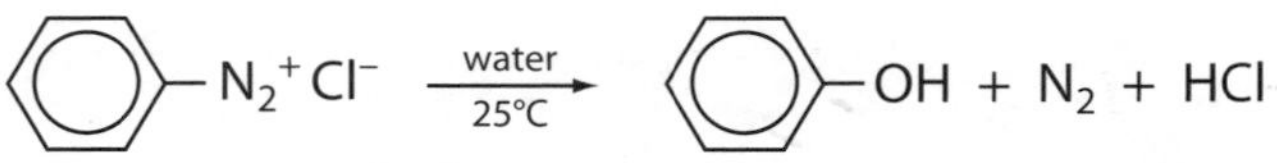

quickfire

㉗ Give the **molecular** formula of the azo dye 4-(phenylazo) phenylamine whose structure is shown in the main text.

quickfire

㉘ What is **seen** when a solution of benzenediazonium chloride at 5°C warms up to room temperature?

Grade boost

The formation of an azo dye needs to be carried out in **alkaline** solution.

Nitrous acid, HNO_2, is not stable enough to be stored at room temperature. Instead, it is made in the reaction from sodium nitrate(III) (sodium nitrite) and an acid, such as dilute hydrochloric acid and used as it is formed.

When an aliphatic amine reacts with nitrous acid at room temperature the products are an alcohol, water and nitrogen gas, which is seen as colourless bubbles in the reaction mixture:

$$CH_3CH_2CH_2NH_2 \ + \ HNO_2 \ \rightarrow \ CH_3CH_2CH_2OH \ + \ N_2 \ + \ H_2O$$
propylamine   propan-1-ol

However, when an aromatic amine is used and the temperature is reduced to around 5°C an intermediate diazonium compound is produced in the solution:

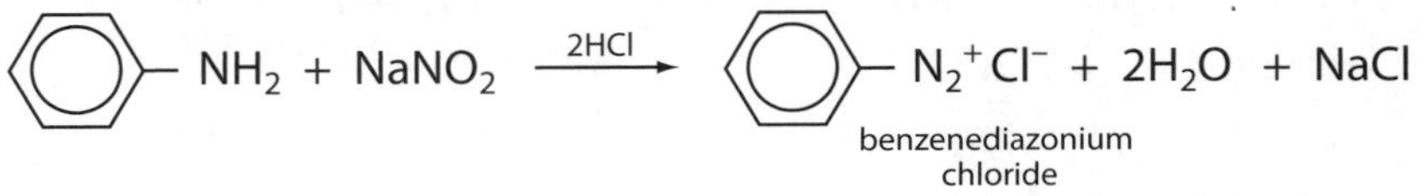

benzenediazonium chloride

These diazonium compounds are very reactive and have many useful reactions. One of these reactions (called a coupling reaction) is the formation of azo dyes, which contain the $-N=N-$ chromophore and this links together two benzene ring systems:

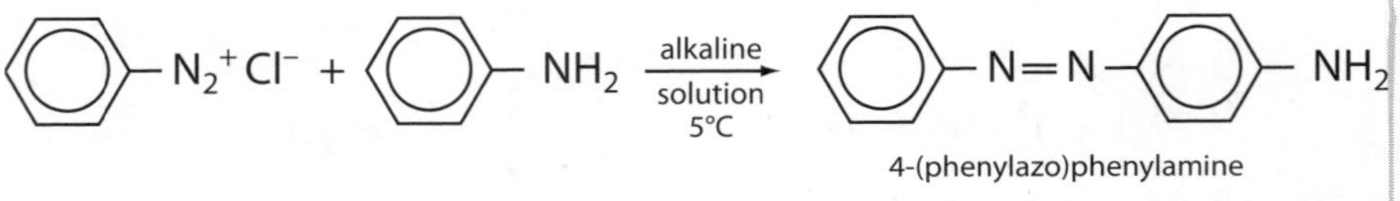

4-(phenylazo)phenylamine

Another example of a coupling reaction is the reaction of benzenediazonium chloride with a phenol such as naphthalene-2-ol:

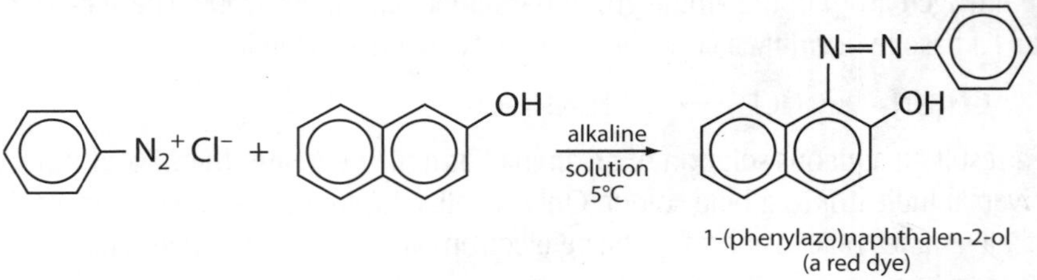

1-(phenylazo)naphthalen-2-ol
(a red dye)

These diazonium compounds are only stable enough to be formed with aromatic amines, and even then the temperature has to be below room temperature. If the temperature of the mixture containing the diazonium compound is allowed to rise to room temperature then decomposition occurs giving the phenol and bubbles of nitrogen gas. In fact, it's the same type of reaction that occurs if we use an aliphatic amine:

α-Amino acids and proteins

The formulae of amino acids

α-Amino acids are carboxylic acids that have an $-NH_2$ group bonded to the carbon atom next to the acid group. The two most common amino acids are aminoethanoic acid (glycine) and 2-aminopropanoic acid (alanine):

$$NH_2 \\ H-C-COOH \\ H$$

aminoethanoic acid
(glycine)

$$H \quad NH_2 \\ H-C-C-COOH \\ H \quad H$$

2-aminopropanoic acid
(alanine)

You should be aware that all α-amino acids, apart from glycine, contain a chiral centre and are therefore optically active. Amino acids have basic ($-NH_2$) and acidic ($-COOH$) groups. They can exist as zwitterions, where a proton is transferred from the acid group to the basic $-NH_2$ group. The zwitterion form of glycine is:

$$^+NH_3 \\ H-C-COO^- \\ H$$

These zwitterions are ionic and the strong attractive forces between positive and negative charges means that α-amino acids have higher melting temperatures than expected if they existed as simple covalent molecules.

The amphoteric nature of α-amino acids

When α-amino acids are dissolved in acidic or alkaline solutions they can gain or lose a proton respectively. As a result α-amino acids are amphoteric substances.

$$NH_2 \\ H-C-COO^- \\ H$$ $\xleftarrow[\text{solution}]{\text{basic}}$ $$^+NH_3 \\ H-C-COO^- \\ H$$ $\xrightarrow[\text{solution}]{\text{acidic}}$ $$^+NH_3 \\ H-C-COOH \\ H$$

The formation of dipeptides

α-Amino acids can react together to form dipeptides that contain the peptide linkage:

$$H \quad O \\ | \quad \| \\ -N-C-$$

If two different α-amino acids are reacted together then two different dipeptides can be formed:

Grade boost

If you are asked to write the displayed formula of a dipeptide or part of a polyamide molecule, make sure that you clearly show the structure of peptide linkage – giving all the bonds.

$$H \quad O \\ | \quad \| \\ -N-C-$$ ✓ $-NHCO-$ ✗

Even if you are giving the structural formula, where all the bonds may not be needed, it is risky to simply write the peptide linkage as: $-NHCO-$.

Make sure too, that you do not give the formula of the same dipeptide twice – just written differently!

quickfire

㉙ The displayed formula of a dipeptide formed from two amino acids is shown below:

$$C_6H_5-C-C-N-C-COOH \\ NH_2 \qquad C_3H_7$$
(with H, O, H, H above the chain)

Write the displayed formula of the other dipeptide formed from these two amino acids.

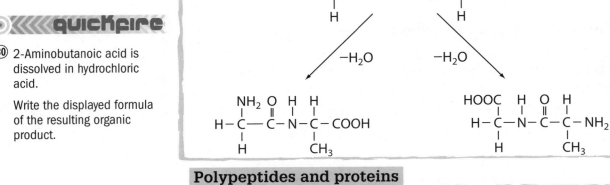

Polypeptides and proteins

This process of peptide formation by the elimination of water (condensation) can continue, to form larger molecules (polypeptides) and can then lead on to the formation of proteins. You need to know about the primary, secondary and tertiary structure of proteins.

Primary structure

This is the sequence of amino acids in the chain.

Secondary structure

This describes the amino acid chains coiling into a double-pleated helix by use of hydrogen bonding, electrostatic attraction and S – S bridges.

Tertiary structure

This describes the resulting overall three-dimensional shape of the protein molecule.

Proteins are extremely important in living systems. Hair, feathers and cartilage are composed mainly of proteins. Some proteins act as enzymes and others act as hormones.

Polyamides

Polyamides are described in more detail in the section on polymers but they are mentioned here as they also contain the peptide linkage:

$$\begin{array}{cc} H & O \\ | & \| \\ -N-C- \end{array}$$

For this specification you are required to know that a polyamide can be made by reacting together a compound with two terminal $-NH_2$ groups, for example 1,6-diaminohexane, $H_2N(CH_2)_6NH_2$, and a compound with two terminal carboxylic acid groups, for example hexane-1,6-dioic acid, $HOOC(CH_2)_4COOH$. Alternatively, molecules of the same compound that contain both an amino group and a carboxylic acid can be condensed together, losing water. An example of this type of compound is 6-aminohexanoic acid, $H_2N(CH_2)_5COOH$.

In industry, different starting materials can be used that are more readily available and more economic to use but you do not need to know these extra details.

Organic synthesis and analysis

Empirical and molecular formulae

The formulae of organic compounds

An organic compound has three basic formulae: the empirical, the molecular and the structural/displayed. Of these, the empirical formula is the simplest, just giving the simplest ratio of atoms present. If the relative molecular mass is known then the molecular formula can be obtained from the empirical formula. The structural/displayed formula gives information about the bonding and functional groups present. Strictly, a displayed formula should show all the bonds, but some allowances are made for OH and NH_2 groups

The empirical formula is often found from the percentage composition values by mass. The molecular formula can then be found by, for example, using mass spectrum molecular ion values, gas volumes or titration data, as appropriate. The following example shows how these formulae can be obtained in an ordered way.

Example 1

A gaseous hydrocarbon contains 85.7% by mass of carbon. 2.10 g of this hydrocarbon occupies a volume of 1.20 dm^3 at room temperature and pressure. Use this information to find the empirical and molecular formulae of the hydrocarbon.

[At room temperature and pressure 1 mole of a gas occupies a volume of 24.0 dm^3.]

Since it is a hydrocarbon (containing C and H only) the % of hydrogen must be $100 - 85.7 = 14.3$

Divide each % by the respective relative atomic mass of the element.

$\quad$ C $\quad 85.7/12.0 = 7.14 \quad\quad$ H $\quad 14.3/1 = 14.3$

Divide each by the smallest value: $\quad$ C $\quad 7.14/7.14 = 1 \quad$ H $\quad 14.3/7.14 = 2$ therefore the empirical formula is C_1H_2 or simply CH_2.

$\quad\quad\quad\quad$ 1.20 dm^3 have a mass of 2.10 g
$\quad$ therefore $\quad$ 1.00 dm^3 has a mass of 2.10/1.20 g
$\quad$ therefore $\quad$ 24.0 dm^3 have a mass of $2.10 \times 24.0/1.20 = 42$ g

therefore the relative molecular mass (M_r) of the hydrocarbon is 42.

$\quad$ 'M_r' of 'CH_2' = 14
$\quad\quad$ n × 14 = 42 $\quad$ where n = number of CH_2 units
$\quad\quad\quad$ thus $\quad$ n = 42/14 = 3
$\quad\quad\quad\quad$ Molecular formula is C_3H_6

You will find another example of this type of calculation in the Question and Answer section later in the book. This calculation uses acid-base titration data to enable you to calculate the relative molecular mass of the monobasic carboxylic acid, RCOOH.

 Grade boost

When you divide the percentages by the relevant relative atomic masses, do not truncate the answers, for example, 1.25 down to 1.0. This practice can easily give misleading results!

The figures provided in the question should give reasonably simple ratios for the empirical formula. If you get a complicated answer then, almost certainly, you have made a mistake in your calculations!

If you arrive at a molecular formula that contains at least six carbon atoms and the number of hydrogen atoms seems relatively small – suspect that it may be an aromatic compound.

 Grade boost

You should always show all your working in calculation questions. This is because an examiner can give you credit even if an error is made at some stage. Just a bare answer that is wrong can gain no credit at all!

Using mass, IR and NMR spectral data in structure determination

Mass spectra

The mass spectrum of an organic compound gives information about the structure of the compound and its relative molecular mass. A mixture of compounds can be separated by gas-liquid chromatography and the individual compounds fed directly into a mass spectrometer. The **molecular ion, M^+** and the fragmentation pattern provide valuable information about the structure of the compound. The simplified mass spectrum of iodoethane is shown below:

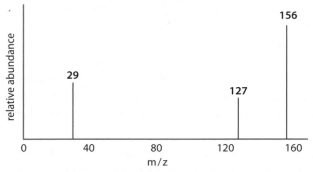

The peak at m/z 156 represents the molecular ion, M_r indicating that its relative molecular mass is 156. There is a peak at 127, which shows the presence of I^+. The difference between 156 and 127 gives 29. The peak at m/z 29 is typical of an ethyl group, $CH_3CH_2^+$. The next simplified mass spectrum is of a chloroalkane. Chlorine consists of two isotopes, ^{35}Cl and ^{37}Cl, present in a 3:1 ratio. A mass spectrum of this compound, which contains only one chlorine atom, will give two molecular ion signals with a difference of 2.

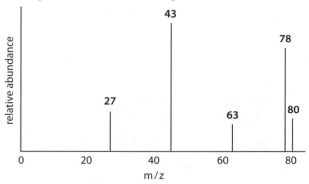

The formula of the chloroalkane is C_xH_yCl. The M_r of the compound with a ^{35}Cl is 78. Therefore the 'M_r' of C_xH_y is 78-35 = 43. This number suggests a $C_3H_7^+$ group. The compound is likely to be 1-chloropropane, CH_3CH_2Cl, or 2-chloropropane, $CH_3CHClCH_3$. As there is no signal at m/z 29 ($CH_3CH_2^+$), it is unlikely to be 1-chloropropane. 2-Chloropropane might be expected to give a peak at 63, if a methyl group is lost and a $CH_3CH^{35}Cl^+$ fragment remains. This is seen in the spectrum, suggesting that the compound is 2-chloropropane.

Infrared (IR) spectra

Each organic compound has its own individual IR spectrum, which gives information about the bonds present in the molecule. For the examination you will be provided with a data sheet that lists characteristic frequencies in wavenumbers (cm^{-1}). You are only required to identify particular bonds in given spectra and to make comments about trends in the intensity of these peaks as the reaction proceeds. Some characteristic values are given in the table.

Bond	Wavenumber/cm^{-1}
C–O	1000–1300
C=C	1620–1670
C=O	1650–1750
C–H	2800–3100
O–H	2500–3550

The IR spectrum of propan-1-ol is given below:

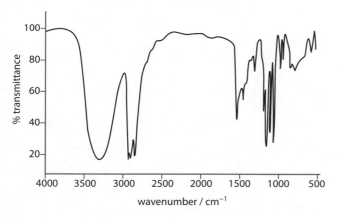

Note the broad peak characteristic of alcohols and carboxylic acids. There is no peak at 1650–1750 cm^{-1}, indicating that a C=O bond is absent; therefore it is likely to be an alcohol.

The next spectrum is a simplified IR spectrum of a compound of molecular formula $C_8H_{16}O_2$:

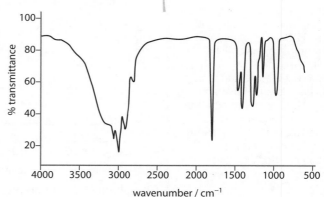

As the compound has two oxygen atoms it is likely to be a carboxylic acid or an ester. The compound fizzes when sodium hydrogencarbonate is added, so it likely to be an acid. Esters do not show an O–H peak at 2500–3500 cm^{-1}. The compound is octanoic acid, $CH_3(CH_2)_6COOH$.

Grade boost

If you are given an IR spectrum, look carefully to see if –OH and/or C=O bonds are present. The presence or absence of these will enable you to distinguish between aldehydes and ketones, alcohols, carboxylic acid and esters.

Pointer

The provided infrared data tends to concentrate on organic compounds containing oxygen, as well as alkenes. Suitable 'unknown' compounds that might be set include alcohols, carboxylic acids, esters as well as aldehydes and ketones.

High resolution NMR spectra = may show split peaks because of the effect of protons that are bonded to neighbouring carbon, oxygen or nitrogen atoms.

» Pointer

If a high resolution NMR spectrum is provided and you see two or more unsplit peaks then these protons are remote from other protons, e.g. as in chloropropanone, $ClCH_2COCH_3$.

Grade boost

If you are given an NMR spectrum and you see a quartet and a triplet – it is almost certainly due to an ethyl group.

If you are given a high resolution spectrum and you a see a single peak, this generally means that there are no hydrogen protons bonded to the neighbouring carbon, oxygen or nitrogen atoms.

» Pointer

It is obvious that this splitting pattern can become very complicated if splitting from 'both sides' occurs. For example, in 1-chloropropane, $CH_3CH_2CH_2Cl$, the middle CH_2 proton signal will be split to a quartet by the CH_3 hydrogen protons and these will be split again by the CH_2Cl hydrogen protons. The examiners will endeavour to find straightforward NMR spectra without this type of complicated splitting pattern.

Nuclear magnetic resonance (NMR) spectra

NMR is concerned with the spin properties of the nucleus. For this specification we are only concerned with the ^1H nucleus (proton). An **NMR spectrum** is obtained when a compound, in a strong magnetic field, is affected by low-energy radio waves. The signal obtained is affected by the environment of the hydrogen atom. For example, the hydrogen protons in ethane, C_2H_6, are all in the same environment, as are all the hydrogen protons in propanone, CH_3COCH_3. However, the single NMR signal for the hydrogen protons in these two compounds will be at different places in the spectrum, as the hydrogen protons in propanone are affected by the C=O group. The usual type of question in the examination requires you to identify various hydrogen protons by use of the provided data sheet. NMR spectra are of two types: low resolution – where only the hydrogen protons bonded to particular atoms are considered and no notice is taken of the influence of neighbouring hydrogen protons; and **high resolution**. The spectrum shows the low resolution spectrum of ethoxyethane. $CH_3CH_2OCH_2CH_3$. The protons are in a ratio of 4:6 (or 2:3) with signals at ~3.5 and 1.2 ppm respectively:

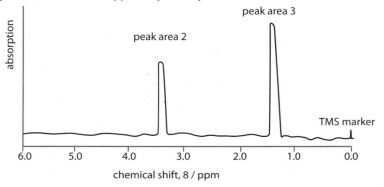

The high resolution spectrum shows that these two signals are again in a ratio of 4:6 but split into a quartet and a triplet respectively:

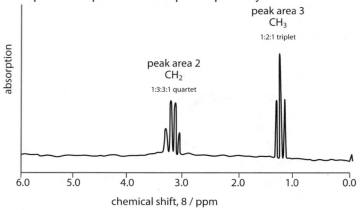

This splitting happens according to the n-1 rule, where n (the number of split peaks in a particular signal) also gives the number of hydrogen protons (atoms) on the neighbouring carbon, oxygen or nitrogen atom.

Basic practical techniques in organic chemistry

Recrystallisation

This is a common technique where both soluble and insoluble impurities can be removed, leaving pure material. The essential stages are:
- Dissolve in the minimum volume of hot solvent
- Filter hot
- Allow to cool
- Filter
- Dry the crystalline product.

Hot filtration removes insoluble impurities. On cooling, the required product will crystallise leaving soluble impurities in solution. After filtering the crystalline solid, it is allowed to dry. This may be on a covered filter paper at room temperature, or in a warm oven set at a temperature below the melting temperature of the pure compound.

Melting temperature

This is used as an indication of the purity of the compound. A pure compound will melt at the temperature given in reference books, perhaps over 1 or 2 degrees. If it is impure then the compound will melt at a **lower** temperature and over a **range** of temperature (perhaps 5 to 10°C or more).

Distillation

This technique can be used to purify liquids. If a mixture of two liquids, which have close boiling temperatures, needs to be separated then fractional distillation is used. A fractionating column enables better separation to occur but the distillation fractions may still be slightly impure. For example, if an ester is made from a carboxylic acid and an alcohol, the distilled ester may still contain traces of the carboxylic acid and water. The acid is then removed by shaking the ester with an aqueous solution of sodium hydrogencarbonate in a separating funnel. The resulting ester will still contain some water and this is removed by using anhydrous calcium chloride or dried magnesium sulfate.

Safety considerations

Many organic compounds are hazardous – many have an appreciable vapour pressure at room temperature. The vapour may be toxic, harmful or irritant, and probably flammable. It is essential to be aware of these potential problems and a detailed risk assessment should be undertaken before work begins. Direct heating using a Bunsen burner is generally undesirable and a hot water bath (suitable for heating up to 100°C) or electrical heating should be used, together with refluxing.

>> *Pointer*

Almost every compound is more soluble in a hot solvent than in the same solvent when cold. This means that a hot **saturated solution** will produce crystalline material on cooling.

quickfire

(31) What would you **see** if you removed traces of acid in an ester by the use of sodium hydrogencarbonate?

Grade boost

In thin layer chromatography the R_f value cannot be greater than 1. If you obtain a value greater then 1, then you have the formula upside down! An R_f value of 1 indicates that the compound is moving at the same rate as the solvent. Another solvent should be tried.

◉◀◀◀◀ quickfire

㉜ You are using GLC. Two compounds appear to have the same retention time. How could you modify the GLC to separate these two compounds?

◉◀◀◀◀ quickfire

㉝ A teacher says that when you carry out TLC you should always have the base line above the solvent in the beaker. Why is this?

Chromatography

You will be familiar with paper chromatography and the specification extends this to include thin layer chromatography (TLC), gas chromatography (GLC) and high performance liquid chromatography (HPLC). The theory of chromatography is not required but you will need to interpret thin layer chromatograms by using retardation factors (R_f values).

Thin layer chromatography

A TLC plate is essentially an absorbent material mounted on a plastic or glass backing plate. As the solution rises up the plate, the mixture will separate into its individual components. Sometimes two compounds travel up the plate to produce a 'spot' that is unresolved. If this happens, using another solvent may separate the two compounds. The R_f value for compound A can be found using the formula:

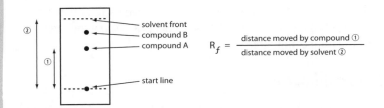

$$R_f = \frac{\text{distance moved by compound } ①}{\text{distance moved by solvent } ②}$$

If compound A is suspected to be a particular compound then a TLC can be taken of the compound, under the same conditions, and the R_f values compared. If the chromatogram consists of colourless spots then spraying with a suitable developing agent, or exposing the chromatogram to UV light may produce coloured spots. Each individual compound can be obtained from the spots by 'removing' the spot and dissolving the 'spot' in a suitable solvent, followed by evaporation.

Gas chromatography

The most common type of gas chromatography is gas-liquid chromatography (GLC), where the gaseous mixture is passed 'through' liquid particles supported on an unreactive solid. The gaseous mixture is carried through the column by an inert gas such as helium. The temperature of the column can be adjusted for effective separation. As each compound emerges from the column it is detected and a peak is observed on the chromatogram. The time taken for the compound to emerge from the column is called the retention time. The relative area of each peak is used to give the % of each compound in the mixture.

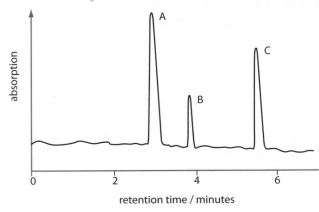

The relative peak areas are shown in the table:

Compound	Relative peak area
A	7.5
B	3.0
C	4.5

The % of compound A = $\dfrac{\text{Relative peak area of compound A} \times 100}{\text{Total peak area}}$

$$= \frac{7.5 \times 100}{15} = 50$$

High performance liquid chromatography

This is a useful technique for separating compounds that cannot be easily vaporised, except at high temperatures, where decomposition may occur. The mixture is injected into a **mobile liquid phase** that is under pressure. The chromatogram obtained is similar in appearance to a GLC chromatogram. A typical application would be to analyse drinking chocolate extract for its caffeine and theobromine content.

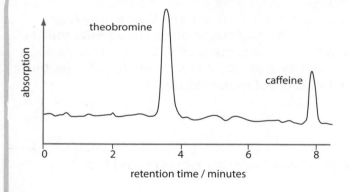

Very often GLC and HPLC columns are linked to other analytical methods. Mixtures are separated by the use of GLC and the separated compounds are fed straight into a mass spectrometer. When the compounds in the mixture are separated using HPLC, the compounds are often fed into ultraviolet/visible spectrophotometers as an aid in compound identification.

Key Term

Radical = a species with an unpaired electron. This could be an atom, e.g. $Cl^•$, or a molecular species, e.g. $^•CH_3$.

Grade boost

It is essential in percentage calculations that you consider the mole ratio of the starting and required materials. Failure to do this will mean the wrong answer and the loss of a valuable mark.

quickfire

㉞ Propanone is converted to propene in a two-stage reaction. State the name of the reagents needed at each stage.

Organic conversions and yields

Organic chemists sometimes need a sequence of reactions to be able to produce a required compound from a particular starting material. Questions on this topic have often proved difficult for candidates, as they need to know a large variety of reactions and to be able to associate the relevant ones together in the correct order. These questions are sometimes combined with the calculation of percentage yields. This is an important consideration if a product is to be made commercially and there are several ways in which it can be made. This topic is best revised by looking at some specific examples.

Example 1

Study the sequence below and give the reagents needed at each stage and any essential conditions:

$$CH_4 \overset{①}{\to} CH_3Cl \overset{②}{\to} CH_3OH \overset{③}{\to} HCOOH$$

In stage 1 substitution has occurred giving chloromethane. This is a radical reaction and **chlorine gas** is needed in the presence of **sunlight.** In stage 2, substitution has again occurred, but this time it is nucleophilic substitution, and methanol is produced by **heating** chloromethane with **aqueous sodium hydroxide**. Finally, in stage 3, the oxidation of an alcohol to a carboxylic acid is occurring. As we have seen previously, the alcohol can be oxidised by **heating** it with an **acidified solution of potassium dichromate**.

Example 2

(a) Study the sequence below and state the names of reagents R and S.

$$\underset{}{NH_2}\text{—}\bigcirc \xrightarrow[20°C]{\text{reagent R}} \underset{}{OH}\text{—}\bigcirc \xrightarrow{\text{reagent S}} \text{2,4,6-tribromophenol}$$

At 20°C phenylamine reacts with **nitrous acid (or sodium nitrite and hydrochloric acid)** (reagent R) to produce phenol. When phenol is treated with aqueous bromine (reagent S) a white precipitate of 2,4,6-tribromophenol is produced.

(b) In an experiment 18.6 g of phenylamine (M_r 93.0) produced 26.5 g of 2,4,6-tribromophenol (M_r 331).

Calculate the **percentage yield** of 2,4,6-tribromophenol.

Number of moles of phenylamine = 18.6/93 = 0.20

Number of moles of 2,4,6-tribromophenol = 26.5/331 = 0.080

The equation shows that 1 mole of phenylamine should give 1 mole of 2,4,6-tribromophenol

% Yield = actual yield x 100/expected yield = $0.080 \times 100 / 0.20 = 40$

Example 3

Study the sequence below and name the reagents (and catalyst where appropriate) used at each stage:

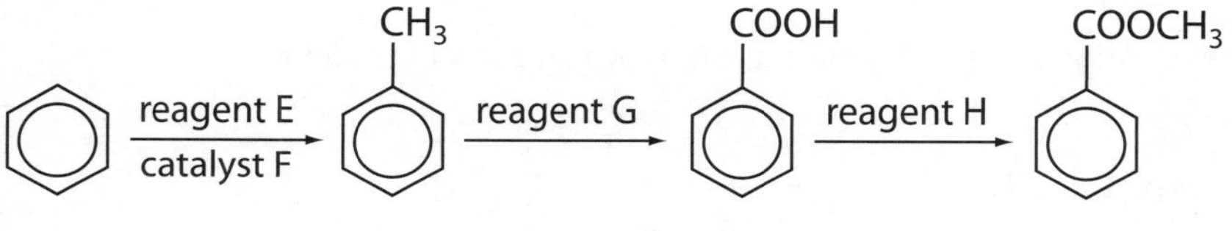

Stage 1 is the **alkylation** of benzene. To introduce alkyl groups we use the Friedel-Crafts reaction. Reagent E is a halogenoalkane, generally chloromethane would be used (sometimes bromomethane is preferred as chloromethane is a gas and the bromo compound is a liquid). The reaction needs a catalyst. The preferred catalyst (Catalyst F), is aluminium chloride, although iron(III) chloride can be used. The next stage of this reaction is the oxidation of a methyl side chain to a carboxylic acid. This oxidation needs fairly drastic conditions. The preferred oxidising agent (Reagent G) is potassium manganate(VII) (or permanganate) used in alkaline solution. The mixture needs too be refluxed for some time. The product of the reaction will be sodium benzenecarboxylate (benzoate) and this needs to be acidified by adding an excess of aqueous hydrochloric acid to the mixture. The next stage is the esterification of the carboxylic acid to give methyl benzenecarboxylate (benzoate). This esterification is carried out by refluxing the acid with methanol (Reagent H) in the presence of a little concentrated sulfuric acid as catalyst.

Key Term

Percentage yield = is given by $\frac{\text{actual yield} \times 100}{\text{theoretical yield}}$.

Alkylation = the introduction of an alkyl group, e.g. methyl or ethyl, into the molecule. This is often met when alkylating aromatic compounds, e.g. methylbenzene from benzene.

quickfire

(35) Ethene is converted to ethanoic acid in a two-stage reaction. State the name of the reagents needed at each stage.

quickfire

(36) A compound, X, reacts with potassium cyanide to give a new compound, Y, which then reacts with lithium tetrahydridoaluminate(III) to give ethylamine. State the names of compounds X and Y.

Grade boost

To obtain the formula of the repeating section of an addition polymer, place the carbon to carbon double bond horizontally and all the attached atoms/groups vertically. Make the double bond into a single bond and place all of the 'structure' into a box with the horizontal bonds 'sticking' out of the box.

quickfire

(37) Use the information in the grade boost above to give the displayed formula of the repeating section of the addition polymer obtained from:
2-chlorobut-1-ene.

quickfire

(38) Write the displayed formula and name the alkene that produces the polymer below:

$$\left[\begin{array}{cc} CH_2Cl & CH_3 \\ | & | \\ -C & -C- \\ | & | \\ H & H \end{array} \right]_n$$

Polymer chemistry

There are two types of polymerisation – addition polymerisation, which you will have met in the AS course, and condensation polymerisation.

Addition polymerisation

In this type of polymerisation **alkene** molecules are added together to form a poly(alkene). The conditions used for this polymerisation depend on the starting alkene, but this radical reaction generally needs increased pressures. An increased pressure is needed for the polymerisation of gaseous alkene molecules so that the 'molecules are closer together and the concentration is higher'. A radical **initiator** (shown below as R−R) is also used – this provides a source of radicals for the initiation stage.

$$R-R \quad \rightarrow \quad 2\,R\bullet$$

The equation for the polymerisation of propene is shown below:

$$n\ CH_3CH = CH_2 \longrightarrow \left[\begin{array}{cc} CH_3 & H \\ | & | \\ -C & -C- \\ | & | \\ H & H \end{array} \right]_n$$

In addition polymerisation a compound with a carbon to carbon double bond produces a polymer where no double bonds are present. The resulting polymer can have varying physical properties, e.g. hardness, softening temperature and tensile strength, depending on the amount of cross-linking between carbon chains and the arrangement of side chain groups. There are no other products (co-products) obtained during addition polymerisation.

Condensation polymerisation

This is a process where molecules react together to form a polymer with the elimination of a small molecule, such as water. The starting compounds contain two functional groups (often bonded to the two end carbon atoms.) Examples of these functional groups include −OH, −NH$_2$ and −COOH groups. Our specification asks us to learn about the production of polyesters and polyamides.

Polyesters

Although there are many polyesters, the specification suggests that we should concentrate on PET. The name PET comes from its older chemical name 'polyethyleneterephthalate'. PET can be made from ethane-1,2-diol and benzene-1,4-dicarboxylic acid.

n HO–C(=O)–⟨benzene ring⟩–C(=O)–OH + n HO–CH₂–CH₂–OH

$-H_2O \longrightarrow$ –C(=O)–⟨benzene ring⟩–C(=O)–O–CH₂–CH₂–O–C(=O)–⟨benzene ring⟩–C(=O)–O–CH₂–CH₂–O–

ester linkage

Key Term

Polyamide = a molecule containing repeating units with peptide linkages at intervals along the chain.

Polyamides

These have already been mentioned in the section on α-amino acids and proteins. You are required to know that they are made by the reaction of a diamine and a dicarboxylic acid. A typical polyester is 'nylon'. There are a number of different **polyamides** that are described as 'nylon'. The number in the nylon 'name' tells us the number of carbon atoms in each molecule of the starting material. For example, Nylon 6,6 is made from 1,6-diaminohexane and hexane-1,6-dioic acid, both of which contain six carbon atoms in their carbon chains:

n $H_2N(CH_2)_6$ NH_2 + n $HOOC(CH_2)_4COOH$

–N(H)(CH₂)₆N(H)–C(=O)(CH₂)₄C(=O)–N(H)(CH₂)₆N(H)–C(=O)(CH₂)₄C(=O)–

peptide linkage

Nylon 6 is slightly more unusual in that it only uses one starting compound, 6-aminohexanoic acid. This compound contains both the $-NH_2$ and the $-COOH$ groups in the same molecule:

n $H_2N(CH_2)_5C$(=O)(OH) $\xrightarrow{-H_2O}$ –[N(H)(CH₂)₅C(=O)–N(H)(CH₂)₅C(=O)]–

peptide linkage

In industry, many polyamides are made using more readily available (and cheaper) starting materials. Our study of polyamides is limited to the details outlined above, however.

Grade boost

Always remember that, to produce a condensation polymer, two different compounds are generally needed, both of which contain two terminal functional groups. Alternatively, one compound with two different functional groups can be used, e.g. $H_2N(CH_2)_3COOH$.

Pointer

Many polyamides are made in industry from readily available cheaper starting materials. You will not be asked about these unless a description is provided in the question 3 case study.

How science works

>> *Pointer*

Questions about this topic will not require a detailed response and the mark allocation will therefore be small. You should, of course, be aware that generally, two marks mean two separate relevant points.

Grade boost

A typical question could involve asking you to compare two processes, having been given suitable data. You should be prepared to comment on the relative merits of one process when compared to the other. This may involve both advantages and disadvantages for both processes.

The work of scientists – methods and validity

Scientists need to be certain that their work can be checked and used by others. So that this can happen they must be confident that their results are accurate, valid and reliable so that their findings can be reproduced by others.

Accuracy

Measurements need to be accurate – this means that they are close to the 'real values'. If students measured the melting temperature of benzenecarboxylic acid (book value 122°C) and found their values to be 120°C, 121°C and 123°C, then their results are described as accurate.

Precision

This is concerned with measurements that are close to each other. If the melting temperature instrument was not calibrated and the students obtained values of 117°C, 118°C and 119°C for benzenecarboxylic acid then these values are precise but not accurate. The values described under accuracy above are both precise and accurate.

Validity

If the data obtained from scientific work is valid then it is correct for the purpose for which it is needed. Factors that should be considered are:

- Has the data been obtained so that it is accurate?
- Have the conclusions been based solely on results and data obtained?
- Is the data relevant to the purpose for which it is being used?

When you are answering questions on this topic you should have an awareness of the methods that scientists use in their work. Recent applications include computational chemistry – this is a branch of chemistry that uses computer science in solving problems in chemistry. Computer programs can be used to calculate the structure and properties of molecules. There is also an increasing interest in the chemistry and uses of nano-sized particles. Another important area is the extraction of pharmacologically active compounds from plants and their synthesis and structure alteration in the laboratory. You should also be aware of considerations that need to be observed before a new product is to be made or a new synthesis is used to make an existing product. These considerations include health and safety in its manufacture and its transport, the availability of starting materials, 'costs', and markets for the product.

Summary: CH4 Analysing and Building Molecules

Spectroscopy

- Chromophores cause colour in organic compounds.
- The colour of organic compounds is due to the colour that is not absorbed.

Isomerism

- Stereoisomerism is concerned with the position atoms and groups take up in space.
- Optically active compounds have a chiral centre.

Aromaticity

- Benzene is stable because of electron delocalisation.
- Many reactions of benzene are electrophilic substitutions.

Alcohols

- Made by the reduction of aldehydes, ketones and carboxylic acids.
- Also made by the hydrolysis of halogenoalkanes and esters.
- Oxidised to aldehydes, ketones and carboxylic acids.
- Give esters with acid chlorides and carboxylic acids.

Phenol

- More acidic than phenols.
- Decolourises aqueous bromine, giving a white precipitate.
- Gives a purple solution with aqueous iron(III) chloride.

Aldehydes and ketones

- Only aldehydes give a silver mirror with Tollens' reagent.
- Both give an orange precipitate with 2,4-dinitrophenylhydrazine.
- Aldehydes can be further oxidised.
- React with hydrogen cyanide by nucleophilic addition.

Carboxylic acids and derivatives

- Lower members are water soluble due to hydrogen bonding.
- Reduced by $LiAlH_4$ to aldehydes and primary alcohols.
- Converted to acid chlorides by PCl_5 and to esters with alcohols.

Nitrogen compounds

- Aliphatic amines formed from halogenoalkanes and ammonia.
- Phenylamine is obtained by reducing nitrobenzene with tin and an acid.
- Diazonium compounds are formed from aromatic amines and nitrous acid at lower temperatures.
- α-Amino acids are amphoteric and exist as zwitterions.
- α-Amino acids condense together to give 'peptides' and proteins.

Organic synthesis and analysis

- For an unknown compound first determine its empirical formula, find the molecular formula and then use chemical reactions and spectroscopy to find its structure.

Polymers

- Addition polymers are made from alkenes.
- Condensation polymers include polyamides and polyesters.

Chromatography

- TLC, HPLC, and gas chromatography are used to separate components from mixtures.

The process of how science works

- Accuracy, reliability and validity are important aspects
- The results should be reproducible.
- Newer developments include computational chemistry and nanotechnology.

CH5 Physical and inorganic chemistry

This unit develops further many aspects of physical and inorganic chemistry seen in units CH1 and CH2. The work relies on the ideas seen in these previous units, and the exam will contain a small number of synoptic questions which test your knowledge and understanding of this earlier work.

The inorganic chemistry work in this unit focuses on the chemistry of the elements of the p-block and d-block, looking at the overarching ideas that affect their properties, and the similarities and differences within the groups of elements.

The physical chemistry work looks at how we can measure the properties of chemical systems and apply the results. Using the ideas of redox reactions, equilibria, rates, enthalpy and entropy we can identify whether chemical reactions are feasible and how industry can ensure that essential chemicals are produced as efficiently as possible. These ideas also allow us to make reliable predictions about chemical reactions that we have not done.

Revision checklist

Tick column 1 when you have completed brief revision notes.
Tick column 2 when you think you have a good grasp of the topic.
Tick column 3 during your final revision for the examination and when you feel that you have mastered the material in the topic.

		1	2	3	Notes
	Redox and electrochemistry				
p49	Redox reactions	✓			
p51	Standard electrode potentials, E^θ				
p53	Redox reactions and titration	✓			
p56	Uses of redox reactions				
	p-block chemistry				
p57	Principles of p-block chemistry				
p59	Group 3				
p61	Group 4				
p63	Group 7				
	d-block transition elements				
p65	d-block transition elements				
p66	Transition metal complexes				
	Chemical kinetics				
p68	Measuring and using reaction rates				
	Enthalpy and entropy				
p71	Enthalpy changes	✓			
p73	Entropy	✓			
	General equilibria				
p75	General equilibria	✓			
	Acid-base equilibria				
p79	Acids and bases	✓			
p82	Buffers	✓			
p83	Acid-base titrations				

Redox and electrochemistry

Redox reactions

In redox reactions something is oxidised and something else is reduced. These processes can be defined in terms of electrons or in terms of oxidation states.

Oxidation states

Oxidation states measure how much an atom has been oxidised compared with the element. Oxidation states allow us to measure **oxidation** and **reduction** in covalent compounds as well as ionic compounds. The oxidation state of an atom is:

- 0 in elements, e.g. in Xe, O_2, C_{60}.
- Equal to the charge in ions, e.g. +2 in Fe^{2+}.
- Negative for the most electronegative atom in a compound.
- +1 for group 1 metals in compounds and +2 for group 2 metals in compounds.
- +1 for hydrogen, except in metal hydrides where it is −1.
- −1 for fluorine in its compounds.
- −2 for oxygen in its compounds except in peroxides where it is −1.
- −1 for halogens in metal halides.

The sum of all the oxidation states of atoms in a compound equals the charge on the species – for a neutral species the sum equals zero.

Oxidation is where oxidation states become more positive; Reduction is where oxidation states become less positive or more negative.

Examples

$$Cr_2O_7^{2-} \ + \ 14\,H^+ \ + \ 6\,Fe^{2+} \ \rightarrow \ 2\,Cr^{3+} \ + \ 6\,Fe^{3+} \ + \ 7\,H_2O$$

Orange   Green

The oxidation state of chromium in the reactants is +6, and in the products it is +3. The chromium has been reduced – we say it is an oxidising agent.

When we add an alkali (e.g. sodium hydroxide) to a solution containing dichromate(VI) ions, the reaction below occurs:

$$Cr_2O_7^{2-} \ + \ 2\,OH^- \ \rightarrow \ 2\,CrO_4^{2-} \ + \ H_2O$$

Orange   Yellow

The oxidation state of chromium in the reactants is +6, and in the products it is +6. It has not been oxidised or reduced – this is not a redox reaction.

Key Terms

Oxidation = loss of electrons OR oxidation state becoming more positive.

Reduction = gain of electrons OR oxidation state becoming more negative.

Grade boost

If you have to identify oxidation or reduction then clearly state the oxidation state of the atom at the start of the reaction and at the end of the reaction and then state whether it has been oxidised (more positive), reduced (more negative) or neither (no change).

Pointer

Oxidising agents become reduced as they oxidise something else.

Reducing agents become oxidised as they reduce something else.

Pointer

Do not mix up charges and oxidation states – they are similar but not the same: +3 and −2 are oxidation states but 3+ and 2− are charges.

quickfire

① Work out the oxidation states of the atoms underlined in the following list: $\underline{S}_8$, $\underline{Fe}^{3+}$, $Na\underline{Cl}$, $H_2\underline{O}$, $F_2\underline{O}$, $Ca\underline{H}_2$, $Al\underline{Cl}_4^-$, $NaO\underline{Cl}$, $Na\underline{I}O_3$, $\underline{Mn}O_4^-$.

>> *Pointer*

Do not mix up a diagram of an electrochemical cell with a cell diagram. A cell diagram is a representation of a cell written in one line of text and not a drawing.

Grade boost

When writing cell diagrams, put the metals at both ends, with a salt bridge in the middle (shown by two vertical lines, ∥). A vertical line shows each change of state, with a comma between species in the same physical state. The metal with the most negative E^{θ} goes on the left.

Equations and half-equations

In a redox reaction, one species is being reduced and another is being oxidised. We can usually divide a full chemical equation into two half-equations, one showing the oxidation and one showing the reduction. In the example below the Cu^{2+} (aq) is being reduced and the Mg (s) is being oxidised:

$$Cu^{2+} (aq) \ + \ Mg (s) \ \rightarrow \ Cu (s) \ + \ Mg^{2+} (aq)$$

The Cu^{2+} (aq) is converted into Cu (s). To do this it must have gained two electrons so the ion-electron half-equation is:

$$Cu^{2+} (aq) \ + \ 2e^{-} \ \rightarrow \ Cu (s)$$

The Mg (s) is converted into Mg^{2+} (aq). To do this it must have lost two electrons so the ion-electron half-equation is:

$$Mg (s) \ \rightarrow \ Mg^{2+} (aq) \ + \ 2e^{-}$$

Electrochemical cells

Half-equations are not just a theory – it is possible to separate a redox reaction so oxidation happens in one place and reduction happens somewhere else. To do this we need to set up two half-cells where the separate processes will happen, and join them together in a complete circuit.

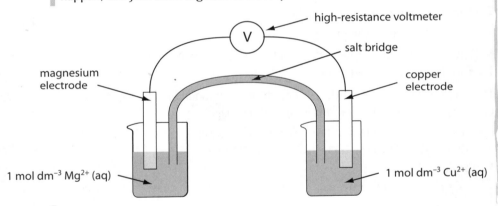

Mg(s)|Mg²⁺ (aq)||Cu²⁺ (aq)|Cu(s) cell

The high resistance voltmeter gives a reading of the EMF produced by the cell. The salt bridge completes the circuit by allowing ions to move, without the two solutions mixing.

Standard electrode potentials, E^θ

Each electrochemical cell has a different tendency to gain or lose electrons, and it is useful to have a way to measure and compare these and so we use the **standard electrode potential (E^θ)**. To measure the value of E^θ for any half-cell, we need to connect it to the standard hydrogen electrode under standard conditions, and measure the potential difference using a high resistance voltmeter.

Standard hydrogen electrode

The standard hydrogen electrode is a half-cell where H_2 gas at a pressure of 1 atm bubbles over an inert platinum electrode dipped in 1 mol dm^{-3} H$^+$ (aq) at a temperature of 298 K.

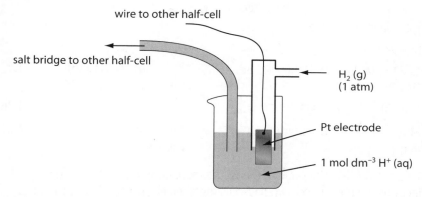

wire to other half-cell

salt bridge to other half-cell

H$_2$ (g) (1 atm)

Pt electrode

1 mol dm^{-3} H$^+$ (aq)

This is the standard half-cell which all others are compared to. Its standard electrode potential is defined as being exactly 0 volts.

We can measure the standard electrode potentials for three types of half-cell:

A metal-solution half-cell: A piece of metal acting as an electrode dipping into a solution containing ions of the same metal. Examples include Cu | Cu^{2+} and Zn | Zn^{2+}.

A gas-solution half-cell: A gas is bubbled over an inert platinum electrode dipping in a solution containing ions of the gas. Examples include the standard hydrogen electrode and X$_2$ (g)|X$^-$ (aq) (X=Cl, Br or I).

A mixed ion half-cell: This half-cell also uses an inert platinum electrode. We place this electrode in a solution containing different ions of the same element in different oxidation states. Examples include Fe^{2+}, Fe^{3+} and Mn^{2+}, MnO$_4^-$. Note that commas are used here as both ions are in the same physical state. A cell diagram for these two half-cells joined together would be Pt | Fe^{2+}, Fe^{3+}|| MnO$_4^-$, Mn^{2+} | Pt.

Key term

Standard electrode potential (E^θ) = the potential difference when any half-cell is connected to the standard hydrogen electrode under standard conditions.

Grade boost

Remember to be clear if you have to label a diagram of a cell – the voltmeter must be a high resistance voltmeter and always specify the metal used to make the electrode. Always include the standard conditions:

- 1 mol dm^{-3} for the concentrations of solutions
- 1 atm for the pressures of gas
- 298K for the temperature.

quickfire

 Draw a labelled diagram to show the electrochemical cell that should be used to measure the standard electrode potential for the following reaction:

Fe^{3+} (aq) + e $\rightarrow$ Fe^{2+} (aq).

Grade boost

quickfire

③ Calculate the standard potentials that would be measured if the following pairs of half-cells were connected together:

1) $Zn \mid Zn^{2+}$ and $Cu \mid Cu^{2+}$.

2) $Zn \mid Zn^{2+}$ and $Fe^{2+}, Fe^{3+} \mid Pt$.

quickfire

④ Use the values of E^{θ} given to show that bromide ions will react with Cl_2 but not with I_2.

Using standard electrode potentials

Some common standard electrode values, along with some of the associated colour changes are listed below:

	E^{θ} / V
Zn^{2+} (aq) $+ 2e^- \rightleftharpoons$ Zn (s)	-0.76
$2 H^+$ (aq) $+ 2e^- \rightleftharpoons H_2$ (g)	0.00
Cu^{2+} (aq) $+ 2e^- \rightleftharpoons$ Cu (s) Blue	$+0.34$
I_2 (aq) $+ 2 e^- \rightleftharpoons 2 I^-$ (aq)	$+0.54$
Fe^{3+} (aq) $+ e^- \rightleftharpoons Fe^{2+}$ (aq) Yellow Pale green	$+0.77$
Br_2 (aq) $+ 2 e^- \rightleftharpoons 2 Br^-$ (aq) Orange Colourless	$+1.09$
$Cr_2O_7^{2-}$ (aq) $+ 14 H^+$(aq) $+ 6e^- \rightleftharpoons 2 Cr^{3+}$ (aq) $+ 7H_2O$(l) Orange Dark green	$+1.33$
Cl_2 (aq) $+ 2 e^- \rightleftharpoons 2 Cl^-$ (aq)	$+1.36$
MnO_4^- (aq) $+ 8 H^+$ (aq) $+ 5e^- \rightleftharpoons Mn^{2+}$ (aq) $+ 4 H_2O$(l) Purple Pale pink/colourless	$+1.51$

The more positive the value of the E^{θ} the more likely the system is to gain electrons. If you connect two half-cells together, electrons will flow from the more negative half-cell to the more positive one. The reading on the high resistance voltmeter will be given by:

Standard potential of cell $= E^{\theta}$ (more positive) $- E^{\theta}$ (less positive)

Is a reaction feasible?

We can use the E^{θ} values to work out if a reaction is feasible. For a reaction to be possible, the EMF for the reaction must be positive. To calculate the EMF, we need to identify which half-equation is the reduction and which is the oxidation.

EMF $= E^{\theta}$ for reduction $- E^{\theta}$ for oxidation

For example, we can identify whether chloride can reduce Cu^{2+} ions to copper metal using the E^{θ} values above. The two relevant half-equations are:

Cu^{2+} (aq) $+ 2e^- \rightleftharpoons$ Cu (s) $\qquad +0.34$ V

Cl_2 (aq) $+ 2 e^- \rightleftharpoons 2 Cl^-$ (aq) $\qquad +1.36$ V

This reaction involves $Cu^{2+} \rightarrow$ Cu, which is a reduction, and $Cl^- \rightarrow Cl_2$, which is an oxidation. The EMF for the reaction is:

EMF $= E^{\theta}$ for $Cu^{2+} - E^{\theta}$ for $Cl^- = 0.34 - 1.36 = -1.02$ V

The reaction is not feasible as the standard potential is negative.

Redox reactions and titration

In a redox reaction both oxidation and reduction occur together, so to work out the overall equation by combining two half-equations, one written as a reduction and one as an oxidation, both equations must contain the same number of electrons.

Example: $Cr_2O_7^{2-}$ reacting with Fe^{2+}.

The two relevant half-equations for this reaction are:

$$Cr_2O_7^{2-} (aq) + 14 H^+(aq) + 6e^- \rightarrow 2 Cr^{3+} (aq) + 7 H_2O (l)$$

$$Fe^{3+} (aq) + e^- \rightarrow Fe^{2+} (aq)$$

Both these are reductions as written above, but as we are starting with Fe^{2+} (aq) rather than Fe^{3+} (aq) we need to reverse the second reaction to make it into an oxidation:

$$Fe^{2+} (aq) \rightarrow Fe^{3+} (aq) + e^-$$

To get the same number of electrons in each we must multiply this by 6 to give:

$$6 Fe^{2+} (aq) \rightarrow 6 Fe^{3+} (aq) + 6 e^-$$

Then we add both equations together, and then cancel out the electrons and anything else that is present in both reactants and products:

$$Cr_2O_7^{2-} + 14 H^+ + 6 e^- + 6 Fe^{2+} \rightarrow 2 Cr^{3+} + 7 H_2O + 6 Fe^{3+} + 6 e^-$$

$$Cr_2O_7^{2-} + 14 H^+ + 6 Fe^{2+} \rightarrow 2 Cr^{3+} + 7 H_2O + 6 Fe^{3+}$$

We must cancel out electrons only, but if there are any other species such as H^+ that are the same on both sides of the equation then these are cancelled out as well.

Redox titrations

You should be familiar with the technique of titration from your previous work in the AS course. Most redox titrations are carried out in the same way as acid-base titrations, except that an indicator is not always needed as the colours of the reactants allow the end point to be seen.

>> **Pointer**

If you need to label a diagram of a cell fully, you'll need to remember that the half-cell with the most positive E^θ value will be the positive electrode, and electrons flow along the wire towards this half-cell.

>> **Pointer**

You do not need to include state symbols like (s) or (aq) unless the question specifically asks you to.

>>>>> **quickfire**

(5) Write a balanced equation for the oxidation of Cl^- by acidified MnO_4^-.

» Pointer

Any calculation from CH1 could appear in the CH5 paper, including interconverting masses and moles, reacting masses, atom economies or percentage yields.

⊙≪≪≪ quickfire

⑥ A 1.252g sample of an iron alloy was dissolved in acid. The Fe^{2+} solution formed required 21.40 cm^3 of potassium manganate(VII) of concentration 0.200 mol dm^{-3} for complete reaction. Calculate the mass of iron present in the alloy. Use this to find the percentage of iron in the alloy.

Oxidation of Fe^{2+} by acidified manganate(VII), MnO_4^-

In the case of a titration involving potassium manganate(VII), this purple solution is added from the burette. When it reacts it forms Mn^{2+}, which is almost colourless. At the end point the solution goes pale pink because some of the purple MnO_4^- remains, which appears pink when dilute.

If we need to do calculations based on a titration like this one, we need to know the reacting ratio (the stoichiometry). This is usually taken straight from the chemical equation. For this titration the equation is:

$$MnO_4^- + 8\,H^+ + 5\,Fe^{2+} \rightarrow Mn^{2+} + 4\,H_2O + 5\,Fe^{3+}$$

This means that the reacting ratio is 1 $MnO_4^- \equiv$ 5 Fe^{2+}.

All titration calculations rely on the same mathematical equations. Since all volumes in titration calculation use volumes of cm^3, the number of moles can be calculated using:

$$\text{Number of moles} = \text{Concentration (in mol dm}^{-3}) \times \frac{\text{Volume (in } cm^3)}{1000}$$

Example question: A solution of Fe^{2+} (aq) is titrated with acidified potassium manganate(VII). A 25.00 cm^3 sample of Fe^{2+} (aq) required 23.80 cm^3 of a potassium manganate(VII) solution of concentration 0.0200 mol dm^{-3} for complete reaction. Calculate the number of moles of Fe^{2+} (aq) present in the sample.

To answer this we need to calculate the number of moles of manganate(VII) using the equation above, then use the reacting ratio to calculate the number of moles of Fe^{2+} (aq) that would react with this.

$$\text{Moles } MnO_4^- = 0.0200 \text{ mol dm}^{-3} \times \frac{23.80 \text{ } cm^3}{1000} = 4.76 \times 10^{-3} \text{ moles}$$

Since 1 $MnO_4^- \equiv$ 5 Fe^{2+} then 4.76×10^{-3} $MnO_4^- \equiv 2.27 \times 10^{-2}$ moles Fe^{2+}

Oxidation of Fe^{2+} by acidified dichromate(VI), $Cr_2O_7^{2-}$

In this reaction, potassium dichromate(VI) turns from orange to green as it oxidises the Fe^{2+}. The reaction is:

$$Cr_2O_7^{2-} + 14\,H^+ + 6\,Fe^{2+} \rightarrow 2\,Cr^{3+} + 7\,H_2O + 6\,Fe^{3+}$$

This means that the reacting ratio is 1 $Cr_2O_7^{2-} \equiv$ 6 Fe^{2+}.

Finding Cu^{2+} by reduction of iodine by thiosulfate, $S_2O_3^{2-}$

We can't measure Cu^{2+} concentration directly but if we add iodide ions to a solution, a white solid of CuI and a brown solution of iodine, I_2 (aq) are formed:

$$2\,Cu^{2+}\,(aq)\ +\ 4\,I^-\,(aq)\ \rightarrow\ 2\,CuI\ +\ I_2$$

We can then add sodium thiosulfate solution from a burette to reduce the iodine:

$$I_2\ +\ 2\,S_2O_3^{2-}\ \rightarrow\ 2\,I^-\ +\ S_4O_6^{2-}$$

This causes the solution to become much paler until it is straw coloured. A starch indicator is then added which is blue-black in the presence of iodine. The end point of the reaction is when the blue-black colour of the starch becomes colourless. We often describe the mixture as appearing flesh-coloured.

We need to work out a reacting ratio that links together Cu^{2+} and $S_2O_3^{2-}$. From the equations above we can see that:

$$2\,Cu^{2+} \equiv 1\,I_2 \qquad \text{and} \qquad 1\,I_2 \equiv 2\,S_2O_3^{2-}$$

We can combine these to show that $2\,Cu^{2+} \equiv 2\,S_2O_3^{2-}$ so $1\,Cu^{2+} \equiv 1\,S_2O_3^{2-}$

quickfire

⑦ An excess of potassium iodide solution was added to 25.00 cm³ of copper(II) sulfate solution, and the iodine released required 30.25 cm³ of a sodium thiosulfate of concentration 0.248 mol dm⁻³ for complete reaction. Calculate the concentration of the copper(II) sulfate solution.

Quick calculations

If you have to calculate a concentration or volume from other volumes and concentrations, you can do this directly using:

$$\frac{C_1 \times V_1}{C_2 \times V_2} = \frac{n_1}{n_2}$$

where C is the concentration, V is the volume and n is the number in the reacting ratio for each substance.

Example question: 25.00 cm³ of a solution of Fe^{2+}(aq) required 24.45 cm³ of a potassium dichromate(VI) solution of concentration 0.0200 mol dm⁻³ for complete reaction. Calculate the concentration of Fe^{2+} (aq) in the solution.

Answer: The reacting ratio in this case is $1\,Cr_2O_7^{2-} \equiv 6\,Fe^{2+}$. Using Fe^{2+} as substance 1 and $Cr_2O_7^{2-}$ as substance 2 we have:

$$\frac{C_{Fe} \times V_{Fe}}{C_{Cr} \times V_{Cr}} = \frac{n_{Fe}}{n_{Cr}} \qquad \text{rearranges to} \qquad C_{Fe} = \frac{n_{Fe} \times C_{Cr} \times V_{Cr}}{n_{Cr} \times V_{Fe}}$$

So: $\quad C_{Fe} = \dfrac{6 \times 0.0200 \times 24.45}{1 \times 25.00} = 0.117$ mol dm⁻³

Uses of redox reactions

Redox reactions are very common in chemistry. You have seen many redox reactions in previous modules, but they are also common in industry, where metals are extracted from their ores; and in biology, respiration and photosynthesis both involve a complex series of reductions and oxidations.

Pointer

Remember that CH5 exams contain synoptic questions, so you can be expected to use redox reactions that you have seen in other modules to answer these questions.

Redox reactions in organic synthesis

You have seen the use of reduction and oxidation in your work in module CH4. These include:

- Oxidation of alcohols to aldehydes, ketones or carboxylic acids using acidified potassium dichromate(VI).
- Reduction of nitriles to amines or reduction of carboxylic acids, aldehydes and ketones to alcohols using lithium tetrahydridoaluminate(III).
- Reduction of nitrobenzene and its derivatives to phenylamines using tin and hydrochloric acid.

Fuel cells

Fuel cells use electrochemical methods to get energy from fuels, typically hydrogen gas. At one platinum electrode, hydrogen is oxidised to H^+ ions, whilst at the other platinum electrode, oxygen gas is reduced to water, H_2O:

At the anode $\qquad\qquad\qquad\qquad H_2 \rightarrow 2H^+ + 2e$

At the cathode $\qquad O_2 + 4H^+ + 4e \rightarrow 2H_2O$

The overall reaction that occurs is: $2H_2 + O_2 \rightarrow 2H_2O$.

This method of obtaining energy has many advantages and disadvantages.

Advantages:

- Water is the only product, so no carbon dioxide (a greenhouse gas) is produced.
- Highly efficient, as less energy is wasted as heat, so much more energy is used effectively.
- Hydrogen gas can be produced using renewable resources by the electrolysis of water.
- Hydrogen can be produced from water, which is a sustainable resource.

Disadvantages:

- Hydrogen gas is highly flammable and difficult to store.
- Hydrogen gas is usually produced from fossil fuels, which leads to a net energy loss.

Grade boost

Make sure you can recall at least one advantage and at least one disadvantage of fuel cells and express these clearly.

Common errors are to use vague answers such as 'less pollution' or 'gases are harmless'.

K *p*-block chemistry

Principles of *p*-block chemistry

The *p*-block is the area of the periodic table where elements have their outermost electrons in *p*-orbitals. You will need to recall and understand the chemistry of groups 3, 4 and 7, and they share some key properties:

- electronic configurations with partially filled *p*-orbitals;
- amphoteric behaviour for some *p*-block metals;
- oxidation states which vary due to octet expansion and the inert pair effect.

>> **Pointer**

When we write 'n' in an electronic configuration we mean the period number so a group 3 element in period 2 would be $2s^2 2p^1$ and for period 4 would be $4s^2 4p^1$.

Electronic configurations

Electronic configurations show how the electrons are arranged in *s*, *p* and *d*-orbitals. The electronic configurations for the *p*-block elements have their outermost electrons in *p*-orbitals. A group 3 element will have a total of three electrons in its *s* and *p*-orbitals, group 4 will have four electrons in these orbitals and group 7 will have seven electrons. These are arranged as shown below.

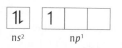

ns^2 np^1

Electronic configuration for group 3

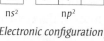

ns^2 np^2

Electronic configuration for group 4

ns^2 np^5

Electronic configuration for group 7

Amphoteric behaviour

Many of the *p*-block metals are **amphoteric**. You are expected to be able to describe chemical reactions that show this, including both observations and equations.

Two examples of amphoteric metals are lead and aluminium. If you add sodium hydroxide to solutions of lead(II) nitrate or aluminium nitrate, you will see a white precipitate that will dissolve when more sodium hydroxide is added, giving a colourless solution.

Reactions of sodium hydroxide with Al^{3+}:

$$Al^{3+}\,(aq) \;+\; 3\,OH^-\,(aq) \;\rightarrow\; Al(OH)_3\,(s)$$

$$Al(OH)_3\,(s) \;+\; OH^-\,(aq) \;\rightarrow\; [Al(OH)_4]^-\,(aq)$$

Reactions of sodium hydroxide with Pb^{2+}:

$$Pb^{2+}\,(aq) \;+\; 2\,OH^-\,(aq) \;\rightarrow\; Pb(OH)_2\,(s)$$

$$Pb(OH)_2\,(s) \;+\; 2\,OH^-\,(aq) \;\rightarrow\; [Pb(OH)_4]^{2-}\,(aq)$$

Key Term

Inert pair = ns^2 pair of electrons not involved in bonding.

Grade boost

You need examples to show octet expansion, e.g. NCl_3 is the only chloride of nitrogen, but phosphorous has two chlorides (PCl_3 and PCl_5) because it has access to d-orbitals to allow for octet expansion.

Pointer

Due to the inert pair effect the elements at the bottom of group 3 have a stable oxidation state of +1.

The elements at the bottom of group 4 have a stable oxidation state of +2.

Those at the bottom of group 5 have a +3 oxidation state.

Oxidation states

The highest oxidation state the p-block elements can reach should equal their group number, so a group 3 element could reach a +3 oxidation state and a group 4 element could reach a +4 oxidation state. Two factors affect whether these elements can reach these maximum values: octet expansion and the **inert pair** effect.

Octet expansion

For compounds in groups 5 or 6 to form their highest oxidation states, they would need 5 or 6 covalent bonds giving 10 or 12 electrons in their outer shell. To fit all these electrons into a shell, we need to use s, p and d-orbitals. This is not a problem for the third period onwards as d-orbitals are available, and we say these elements can form more bonds because they can expand their octet by using the d-orbitals.

The second period elements (N and O) don't have any d-orbitals so we say these elements cannot expand their octets, so they can only have 8 electrons in their outer shells. This limits nitrogen to three covalent bonds and oxygen to two covalent bonds.

Inert pair effect

All the p-block elements have a pair of electrons in the s-orbital, as well as electrons in their p-orbitals and most of the elements use all these electrons during bonding. As you go down the groups, the ns^2 pair of electrons are less able to be involved in bonding, and we call them an inert pair.

This makes the elements lower in the group show an oxidation state 2 lower than the group number. The stability of the lower oxidation state becomes greater as you go down the group.

Group 3

Group 3 elements have three electrons in their outer shell, and these are arranged as ns^2np^1. The first two members of the group are boron and aluminium, and you only need to know about the chemistry of these two elements.

Electron deficiency

All group 3 elements have three outer electrons, and this allows them to form three covalent bonds to make compounds where they are electron-deficient. Common examples of **electron-deficient** group 3 compounds are BF_3, BCl_3 and $AlCl_3$. A lot of the chemistry of group 3 compounds is based around reactions with species with **lone pairs**, as this removes the electron deficiency by forming a **co-ordinate bond**.

Aluminium chloride

The aluminium atom in $AlCl_3$ is electron-deficient, and the chlorine atoms have three lone pairs each. This allows co-ordinate bonds to form between a chlorine atom of one $AlCl_3$ and the aluminium atom of another, with two co-ordinate bonds between $AlCl_3$ monomers forming a **dimer**.

Aluminium chloride can also form a co-ordinate bond with a chloride ion to form the tetrachloroaluminate ion, $AlCl_4^-$. The formation of these ions is important in two areas of chemistry.

Chlorination of benzene

$AlCl_3$ is used as a halogen carrier to create a positively charged chlorine electrophile in the chlorination of benzene, as shown below. The $AlCl_3$ is called a 'halogen carrier'.

Ionic liquids

These are ionic compounds which are liquids at room temperatures or just above, and they usually contain $AlCl_4^-$ anions and large organic cations. They are being developed as solvents and catalysts for reactions such as polymerisation of alkenes. They make it much easier to separate the products from the reactants and solvent, and their low volatility means the liquid doesn't evaporate during use.

Key Terms

Co-ordinate bond = shared pair of electrons, both from the same atom.

Dimer = a species created when two molecules join together.

Electron-deficient = a species with fewer than eight electrons in its outer shell, so this shell is not full.

Lone pair = pair of electrons in an outer shell that are not involved in bonding.

Structure of Aluminium chloride dimer

Bonding in Aluminium chloride dimer

Grade boost

Make sure you can recall some advantages of ionic liquids.

Key Term

Isoelectric = same number of electrons in the outer shell.

Grade boost

Make sure you can recall the properties of graphite and boron nitride, and can link these to their structures.

Donor-acceptor compounds

The boron atom in BF_3 is electron-deficient, and like $AlCl_3$ it will try to react with molecules with lone pairs, such as NH_3, to get rid of the electron deficiency. These compounds are called donor-acceptor compounds because the NH_3 donates a lone pair to the bond that is made, and the BF_3 accepts it. Similar compounds can be formed from any electron-deficient group 3 compounds.

Structure of donor-acceptor compound (Structure of $NH_3.BF_3$)

Bonding in donor-acceptor compound (Bonding in $NH_3.BF_3$)

Boron nitride

Boron nitride, BN, is **isoelectronic** with carbon and so it forms similar structures to the allotropes of carbon: graphite, diamond and nanotubes.

Hexagonal boron nitride

This has a similar structure to graphite with layers of hexagons formed by covalent bonds between atoms. The main difference between them is that the hexagons in boron nitride have the atoms lying above one another, whilst in graphite the atoms in adjacent layers do not lie above one another.

Both hexagonal boron nitride and graphite are soft because the forces between the layers are weak so the layers can slide over one another. Boron nitride differs from graphite as it is an insulator whilst graphite is an electrical conductor. Both materials can be used as lubricants, but the difference in electrical conductivity and relative inertness allows boron nitride to be used where graphite could not be.

Cubic boron nitride

This has a similar structure to diamond with a tetrahedral arrangement of boron atoms around nitrogen atoms and vice versa. It is one of the hardest materials known with a high melting temperature, and is an excellent heat conductor and chemically unreactive. These properties make it ideal for mounting high power electronic components, as wear-resistant coatings and as supports for catalysts.

Boron nitride nanotubes

A layer of hexagonal boron nitride can be used to wrap around carbon nanotubes. The boron nitride acts as an insulating layer around the conducting carbon nanotube to keep the current within the nanotube.

Group 4

In group 4, we study the differences between the elements, especially those at the top and bottom of the group. The differences are significant and are usually linked to the increase in metallic character down the group or the increasing stability of the +2 oxidation state.

Metal/non-metal properties

The elements at the top of group 4, carbon and silicon, are non-metals which have giant covalent structures. The two elements at the bottom of the group are tin and lead, and these are both metals so they have metallic bonding with lattices of positive metal ions in a sea of delocalised electrons.

Oxidation states

The maximum oxidation state in group 4 is +4, but the inert pair effect becomes more significant down the group, so the lower elements in the group have a +2 oxidation state as well.

Carbon is stable in an oxidation state of +4, and only exists as +2 in CO. This means that CO will act as a reducing agent as it tries to reach the stable +4 oxidation state. CO is used in the extraction of metals from their oxides, with the extraction of iron being the most common example:

$$Fe_2O_3 \ + \ 3\,CO \ \rightarrow \ 2\,Fe \ + \ 3\,CO_2$$

Tin is also stable in the +4 oxidation state, so tin(II) compounds are reducing agents, such as in the reduction of nitrobenzene in module CH4.

Lead has compounds with both +4 and +2 oxidation states, such as PbO_2 and PbO. The +2 oxidation state is more stable, and so lead(IV) compounds are oxidising agents. An example of this is:

$$PbO_2 \ (s) \ + \ 4\,HCl\ (conc.) \ \rightarrow \ PbCl_2 \ (s) \ + \ Cl_2 \ (g) \ + \ 2\,H_2O \ (l)$$

Group 4 oxides and chlorides

At the top of group 4, the elements are non-metals, and so they use covalent bonding. In the case of CO_2, CCl_4 and $SiCl_4$ the compounds have simple molecular structures, with CO_2 being a gas and CCl_4 and $SiCl_4$ being liquids.

Lead(II) oxide and lead(II) chloride both use ionic bonding, and adopt giant ionic structures. These compounds are both solids.

Grade boost

Tin and lead show +2 and +4 oxidation states. In Tin +4 is the most stable, but in lead +2 is the most stable.

quickfire

⑧ Carbon monoxide can be used as a reducing agent whilst PbO cannot. Explain this difference.

Grade boost

Two metal ions form a yellow precipitate with iodide ions – silver and lead(II). This observation is regularly used in questions to identify these metals.

quickfire

⑨ Explain how sodium hydroxide solution can be used to distinguish between solutions of magnesium nitrate and lead(II) nitrate.

Acid-base properties of oxides

Carbon dioxide is an **acidic oxide** so it reacts easily with bases.

$$2\,NaOH\,(aq)\ +\ CO_2\,(g)\ \rightarrow\ Na_2CO_3\,(aq)\ +\ H_2O\,(l)$$

Like most *p*-block metal oxides, lead(II) oxide is an amphoteric oxide so it reacts with both acids and bases to form colourless solutions.

Reaction with an acid:

$$PbO\,(s)\ +\ 2\,HNO_3\,(aq)\ \rightarrow\ Pb(NO_3)_2\,(aq)\ +\ H_2O\,(l)$$

Reaction with a base:

$$PbO\,(s)\ +\ 2\,NaOH\,(aq)\ +\ H_2O\,(l)\ \rightarrow\ Na_2[Pb(OH)_4]\,(aq)$$

Reactions of chlorides with water

Most covalent chlorides react with water, so when $SiCl_4$ is added to water, the two liquids react very quickly, forming a white solid (SiO_2) and bubbles which release steamy fumes of HCl:

$$SiCl_4\ +\ 2\,H_2O\ \rightarrow\ SiO_2\ +\ 4\,HCl$$

When CCl_4 is added to water it does not react, it forms a separate colourless liquid layer. This difference is due to the presence of *d*-orbitals in the outer shell of silicon, which are not present in carbon. These *d*-orbitals allow a lone pair from oxygen to bond to the silicon of the $SiCl_4$ to start the reaction. As carbon has no *d*-orbitals, it cannot react.

Ionic chlorides like $PbCl_2$ do not react with water, and as $PbCl_2$ is insoluble it will remain as a white solid when mixed with water.

Reactions of Pb^{2+}

Most compounds of Pb^{2+} are insoluble, with lead(II) nitrate and lead(II) ethanoate being the only common soluble compounds. Adding other solutions to a solution containing Pb^{2+} (aq) ions usually causes a precipitate to form.

Ions added	Observation	Precipitate
OH^- (aq)	White precipitate	Lead(II) hydroxide, $Pb(OH)_2$
Excess OH^- (aq)	Precipitate dissolves to form colourless solution	Tetrahydroxoplumbate(II), $[Pb(OH)_4]^{2-}$
Cl^- (aq)	White precipitate	Lead(II) chloride, $PbCl_2$
I^- (aq)	Bright yellow precipitate	Lead(II) iodide , PbI_2

The precipitation reactions follow the same general ionic equation:

$$Pb^{2+}(aq)\ +\ 2\,X^-\,(aq)\ \rightarrow\ MX_2\,(s)$$

Lead is an amphoteric metal, and so the white precipitate dissolves in excess sodium hydroxide solution according to the ionic equation:

$$Pb(OH)_2\ +\ 2\,OH^-\ \rightarrow\ [Pb(OH)_4]^{2-}$$

Group 7

You should be familiar with a lot of group 7 chemistry from GCSE and your year 12 work. This will include the physical appearance of the elements and the tests for chloride, bromide and iodide ions using silver nitrate.

Patterns in group 7 reactions

When studying the reactions of this group, the key factor is often the stability of different oxidation states. Standard electrode potentials, E^θ, are a measure of how good the elements are at oxidising other substances.

	E^θ / Volts
$Cl_2\,(aq) + 2e^- \rightleftharpoons 2\,Cl^-(aq)$	+1.36
$Br_2\,(aq) + 2e^- \rightleftharpoons 2\,Br^-(aq)$	+1.09
$I_2\,(aq) + 2e^- \rightleftharpoons 2\,I^-(aq)$	+0.54

Chlorine is the most oxidising, and iodine is the least oxidising of the three. This shows that the −1 oxidation state of chlorine is more stable than the −1 oxidation state of bromine or iodine.

Displacement reactions

During CH2, you studied the displacement reactions of the halogens where a more reactive halogen oxidises the ions of a less reactive one, such as chlorine displacing bromide ions:

$$Cl_2\,(g) + 2\,Br^-\,(aq) \rightarrow 2\,Cl^-\,(aq) + Br_2\,(aq)$$

In terms of standard electrode potentials (E^θ) we can show that because chlorine has a more positive E^θ than bromide, chlorine is a stronger oxidising agent and will oxidise bromide to bromine. You need to be able to explain the oxidation of iodide by chlorine or by bromine in a similar way.

Reaction of chlorine with sodium hydroxide

Chlorine reacts with dilute sodium hydroxide in one of two ways, depending on the temperature used. In the cold they make sodium chloride, NaCl, and sodium chlorate(I), NaOCl. This is a **disproportionation** reaction, with chlorine having a −1 oxidation state in NaCl and +1 in NaOCl:

$$Cl_2 + 2\,NaOH \rightarrow NaCl + NaOCl + H_2O$$

When heated, a different reaction occurs to produce sodium chloride, NaCl, and sodium chlorate(V), $NaClO_3$. Once again this is a disproportionation reaction, with chlorine having a −1 oxidation state in NaCl and +5 in $NaClO_3$:

$$Cl_2 + 6\,NaOH \rightarrow 5\,NaCl + NaClO_3 + 3\,H_2O$$

Key Term

Disproportionation = a reaction where atoms of the same element become oxidised and reduced to form two different products.

》Pointer

When discussing oxidation and reduction, make sure you are clear and say iodide is a reducing agent, while iodine is an oxidising agent.

Pointer

You need to recall the products and observations for the reactions of concentrated sulfuric acid with NaCl, NaBr and NaI but you do not need to write equations for these reactions.

Grade boost

When asked for a use of chlorine then a use of the element is needed.

When asked for a use of a chlorine compound, then chlorine itself is not appropriate.

quickfire

(10) List the sulfur-containing products of the reaction of NaI with concentrated sulfuric acid, giving the associated observation where possible.

Reaction of sodium halides with concentrated sulfuric acid

When you add concentrated sulfuric acid to any sodium halide, NaX, the same initial chemical reaction occurs, whether the halide is NaCl, NaBr or NaI. This reaction produces steamy fumes of HX gas:

$$NaX + H_2SO_4 \rightarrow NaHSO_4 + HX$$

For NaCl, this is the only reaction that occurs, but HBr and HI react further because bromide and iodide have lower E^θ values, so it is easier to oxidise these halides.

HBr can be oxidised by the sulfuric acid to form Br_2 as orange fumes. During the process the sulfur in $NaHSO_4$ is reduced from +6, and forms SO_2 with an oxidation state of +4. The bromide is a strong enough reducing agent to reduce sulfur from +6 to +4.

HI can be oxidised by the sulfuric acid to form I_2 as a black solid or purple fumes. During the process the sulfur in $NaHSO_4$ is reduced from +6, and forms SO_2 with an oxidation state of +4, S as a yellow solid (oxidation state 0) and H_2S as a gas which smells of rotten eggs (oxidation state −2). The iodide is a much stronger reducing agent and can reduce sulfur from +6 to −2.

Uses of halogens and their compounds

- Chlorine is used in the disinfection of water supplies.
- Sodium chlorate(I), NaOCl contains ClO^- ions which kill bacteria and act as a bleach. This is because they are strong oxidising agents, and the oxidation of dyes forms colourless compounds and the oxidation of biological molecules in the bacteria kills them. Chlorine gas acts in a similar way.
- Sodium chlorate(V), $NaClO_3$, is used as a weed killer.
- Polytetrafluoroethene (PTFE) is used as a non-stick layer on frying pans and bearings.
- Poly(chloroethene) (PVC) is a polymer used as waterproof coatings and for window frames.
- Trichlorophenol (TCP) is used as an antiseptic.
- Silver bromide is used in traditional photographic film.
- Iodine is used as an antiseptic.

d-block transition elements

d-block transition elements

The elements of the *d*-block are classed as **transition elements** if they have partially filled *d*-orbitals in their atoms or their ions. They share some key properties that you need to recall and explain:

- They have several different oxidation states.
- They form complexes by co-ordinate bonding; which are usually coloured.
- Both the metals themselves and their compounds can act as catalysts.

Electronic configurations

Electronic configurations show how the electrons are arranged in *s*, *p* and *d*-orbitals. The inner shells are full and contain 18 electrons, and these are arranged as $1s^2\ 2s^22p^6\ 3s^23p^6$. The outer electrons are in the 3*d* and 4*s* orbitals — remember that the 4*s* orbital is filled before the 3*d* orbitals.

3*d*³   4*s*²

3*d*⁶   4*s*²

Electronic configuration of vanadium   *Electronic configuration of iron*

Transition metal ions

When you write the electronic configuration for transition metals ions, remember that the atoms lose 4*s* electrons before the 3*d* electrons. This means the 4*s* orbital is empty in all the transition metal ions.

 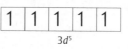

3*d*²   4*s*⁰

3*d*⁵   4*s*⁰

Electronic configuration of V³⁺   *Electronic configuration of Fe³⁺*

Oxidation states

The ionisation energies for electrons in *d*-orbitals are all similar, which causes each transition metal to have a variety of different oxidation states. You need remember the common oxidation states of some common metals:

- Chromium: +3 and +6
- Manganese: +2, +4 and +7
- Iron: +2 and +3
- Copper: +1 and +2

Key Terms

Ligand = a small molecule with a lone pair that can bond to a transition metal ion.

Complex = ligands joined to a transition metal by co-ordinate bonds.

Monodentate (not in text but important) = ligand that has one atom that can bond to a metal ion.

Bidentate (not in text but important) = ligand that has two atoms that can bond to a metal ion.

Grade boost

When you draw the complexes, remember to use wedge and dotted lines to show the three-dimensional structure, with the bonds going to the atom with the lone pair.

≫ Pointer

Not all complexes are coloured. If a transition metal ion has filled d-orbitals (e.g. Cu^+) or empty d-orbitals (e.g. Sc^{3+}, Ti^{4+}) then electrons cannot move from the lower energy level to the higher one.

Transition metal complexes

Complexes are made up of a transition metal ion bonded to atoms or molecules which surround it. There are empty orbitals on the metal ion and the ligands have lone pairs so they can form co-ordinate bonds together. The complexes usually have six **ligands** and an octahedral shape, although some have four ligands and a tetrahedral shape. Typical ligands include water (H_2O), ammonia (NH_3) and chloride (Cl^-).

Examples of complexes

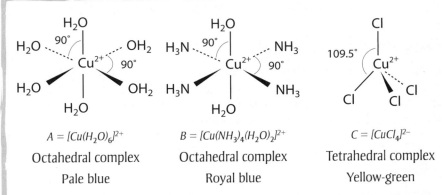

$A = [Cu(H_2O)_6]^{2+}$
Octahedral complex
Pale blue

$B = [Cu(NH_3)_4(H_2O)_2]^{2+}$
Octahedral complex
Royal blue

$C = [CuCl_4]^{2-}$
Tetrahedral complex
Yellow-green

If you dissolve a transition metal compound in water, the water molecules act as ligands and usually form octahedral complexes such as complex A. To turn complex A into one of the others, you need to add a solution that contains a new ligand – adding ammonia solution forms complex B, whilst adding concentrated hydrochloric acid forms complex C.

Colour of complexes

Transition metal ions are only coloured when they form complexes. In a transition metal ion, all the d-orbitals have the same energy level but when it forms a complex this causes the d-orbitals to split into two sets – 3 lower energy and 2 higher energy orbitals.

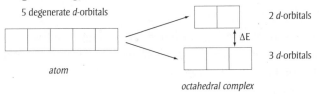

For electrons to move from the lower energy level to the higher energy they must absorb the correct amount of energy, ΔE. This energy corresponds to one specific frequency of light, as $\Delta E = hf$. The colour seen is the made up of the frequencies of light which are not absorbed. Different ligands cause different splitting of the d-orbitals, so different frequencies are absorbed and this gives different colours.

Reactions with sodium hydroxide

Many transition metal compounds form coloured solutions. If you add sodium hydroxide solution to these solutions, you will see a coloured precipitate. If you add even more sodium hydroxide until you have an excess, some precipitates can dissolve again to form a coloured solution.

	Colour of solution	Observation with NaOH (aq)	Observation with excess NaOH (aq)
Chromium(III), Cr^{3+}	green	grey-green precipitate	green solution
Iron(II), Fe^{2+}	pale green	dark green precipitate	no change
Iron(III), Fe^{3+}	yellow	red-brown precipitate	no change
Copper(II), Cu^{2+}	blue	pale blue precipitate	no change

These precipitation reactions follow one of two general ionic equations:

$$M^{2+}(aq) + 2\,OH^-(aq) \rightarrow M(OH)_2(s)$$
$$M^{3+}(aq) + 3\,OH^-(aq) \rightarrow M(OH)_3(s)$$

The reaction of excess sodium hydroxide with $Cr(OH)_3$ follows the equation:

$$Cr(OH)_3 + 3\,OH^- \rightarrow [Cr(OH)_6]^{3-}$$

Uses of transition metals

Catalysts

Transition metal atoms and ions can act as catalysts because they have partially filled *d*-orbitals and variable oxidation states. This allows them to bond to reactant molecules and then oxidise or reduce these to make them far more reactive. Examples of catalysts include:

- Vanadium(V) oxide – contact process for production of sulfuric acid.
- Titanium chloride – polymerisation of ethene.
- Iron – Haber process for production of ammonia.
- Nickel or platinum – catalytic hydrogenation of alkenes.

Biological systems

The transition metals are present in trace amounts in many biological systems, including:

- Iron – present in haemoglobin which carries oxygen around the body.
- Cobalt – a component of vitamin B_{12}.

Economic importance

- Chromium – a component of stainless steel.
- Iron – used in iron and steel manufacture for construction.
- Copper – used in circuitry and electronics.

Grade boost

When you are describing the observations when sodium hydroxide is added to a solution, give the colour of the original solution and the colour of the precipitate. If the precipitate dissolves with excess sodium hydroxide, give the colour of the solution formed.

quickfire

(12) Write ionic equations for the reactions with sodium hydroxide solution of Cu^{2+} and Fe^{3+}.

≫ Pointer

Copper(II) hydroxide is also formed when aqueous ammonia solution is added to copper(II) compounds in solution. It then reacts further to form a solution of the royal blue complex $[Cu(NH_3)_4(H_2O)_2]^{2+}$.

≫ Pointer

Make sure you can recall at least one example from each category of the uses.

Chemical kinetics

Measuring and using reaction rates

Chemical kinetics is the study of the rates of chemical reactions and how they change. When measuring a reaction rate, we measure one factor as it changes over a period of time. Common methods of measuring rates are:

- Colourimetry – used when a coloured substance is created or used up during a chemical reaction.
- Measurement of gas volume (at constant pressure) with a gas syringe – used when a gas is produced in a chemical reaction.
- Measurement of mass – used when a gas is released in a chemical reaction.
- Measurement of gas pressure (at constant volume) – used for a reaction where reactants and products are gases and the number of gas molecules changes.

Calculating rates

You can calculate rates from numerical values or graphs. If you are given values then you need to divide the change in amount of substance or concentration by the time taken.

Time(s)	Concentration of reactant (mol dm^{-3})
0	1.50
60	1.20

$$Rate = \frac{change}{time} = \frac{(1.20 - 1.50)}{60} = -5.0 \times 10^{-3}\,mol\,dm^{-3}s^{-1}$$

If these are drawn as graphs, you need to draw a tangent to the curve and calculate its gradient in a similar manner to above.

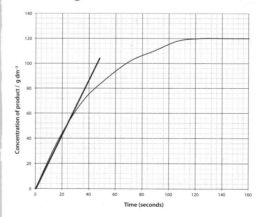

$$Rate = \frac{change}{time} = \frac{44}{20} = 2.2g\,dm^{-3}\,s^{-1}$$

Iodine clock

A clock reaction shows a sudden change when the reaction has reached a certain point, and we measure the time this takes. The most common clock reaction is the iodine clock, where the iodine produced changes the solution black due to the starch indicator used.

The rate of a clock reaction is calculated by dividing one by the time taken: if the clock reaction changes after 20 seconds, then the rate is $1 \div 20 = 0.05$ s^{-1}.

Orders of reaction

The rate of a chemical reaction will depend on the concentrations of the reactions, but this is not always a simple proportional relationship. When the concentration of one reactant (shown as [A]) is doubled, scientists have found that the rate of the reaction may be:

Unchanged	Rate is not dependent on concentration	rate $\propto [A]^0$
× 2	Rate is proportional to concentration	rate $\propto [A]^1$
× 4	Rate is proportional to concentration squared	rate $\propto [A]^2$

You can only work out the order from rate data, and not from the chemical equation. If you look at the table of data below, you can work out the order with respect to Br_2 and the order with respect to alkene from an experiment where an alkene was reacted with Br_2.

	$[Br_2]$ / mol dm^{-3}	[alkene] / mol dm^{-3}	Rate / mol dm^{-3} s^{-1}
1	1.0×10^{-3}	6.0×10^{-3}	0.5×10^{-3}
2	2.0×10^{-3}	6.0×10^{-3}	2.0×10^{-3}
3	6.0×10^{-3}	1.0×10^{-3}	3.0×10^{-3}
4	6.0×10^{-3}	2.0×10^{-3}	6.0×10^{-3}

We need to find two sets of data where only one concentration changes. In this case we can use lines 1 and 2 where the concentration of Br_2 changes but the concentration of the alkene stays the same. As the concentration of Br_2 doubles, the rate increases by a factor of 4, which means that the reaction is second order with respect to Br_2.

Looking at lines 3 and 4, the concentration of the alkene changes but the concentration of Br_2 stays the same. As the concentration of alkene doubles, the rate increases by a factor of 2, which means that the reaction is first order with respect to alkene.

Rate equation

From this information, you can build up an overall rate equation. For the reaction above: rate = $k [Br_2]^2[alkene]^1$, k is called the rate constant.

^{2} is the order of the reaction with respect to Br_2, and ^{1} is the order of the reaction with respect to alkene. The overall order of the reaction is the sum of the individual orders, 3 in this case.

Rate determining step
= the slowest step in a
reaction mechanism.

quickfire

⑮ Give the order of the following
reactions and the units of the
rate constant in each case:

(i) Rate = k [HI] [Cl_2]

(ii) Rate = k [O_3]

quickfire

⑯ Write a rate equation for
a reaction that has the
following rate determining
step:

$N_2O_5 + H_2O \longrightarrow 2HNO_3$

quickfire

⑰ Suggest a rate determining
step for the alkaline
hydrolysis of bromobutane
which has the following rate
equation:

Rate = k [C_4H_9Br] [OH^-]

Rate constants

This is a constant in the rate equation. It is constant for a given reaction at a
particular temperature, and is not affected by changing the concentrations of
the reactants but changes if we change temperature or add a catalyst. The rate
of a reaction in solution is typically quoted as mol dm^{-3} s^{-1}: This is the change
in concentration (mol dm^{-3}) per second. The rate constant has to have units for
the units in the equation to balance.

Order	Rate equation	Units of k
Zeroth	Rate = k	mol dm^{-3} s^{-1}
First	Rate = k [A]	s^{-1}
Second	Rate = k [A]^2	mol^{-1} dm^3 s^{-1}

Rates and mechanisms

The mechanism of a reaction is the series of steps that happen during a
chemical reaction. The rate equation provides important information about one
of these steps – this is the slowest step, which we call the **rate determining
step**. The substances in the rate equation correspond to the reactants in the
rate determining step and their orders correspond to the balancing numbers in
the equation.

Examples

Rate = k [N_2O_4] so the rate determining step must start $N_2O_4 \rightarrow$

Rate = k [NO]^2 so the rate determining step must start 2 NO

Rate = k [H_2][I_2] so the rate determining step must start $H_2 + I_2 \rightarrow$

If the rate determining step is $O_3 + Cl^- \rightarrow O_2 + OCl^-$ then Rate = k [O_3][Cl^-]

Effect of temperature on rates and equilibria

It is easy to confuse the ideas of rates and equilibria; however, the effect of
changing temperature on each can be very different. Raising the temperature
always increases the rate of reaction. In terms of the rate equation, it increases
the value of rate constant.

For equilibria, raising the temperature may:

- Increase the amounts of product in an equilibrium mixture (for an
  endothermic reaction).

- Reduce the amounts of product in an equilibrium mixture (for an exothermic
  reaction).

Enthalpy and entropy

Enthalpy changes

Many enthalpy changes have special names, and you need to be familiar with these, although you will not have to give formal definitions.

Enthalpy change of atomisation: This is the enthalpy change to form one mole of atoms in the gas phase. For example:

$$Na\,(s) \quad \rightarrow \quad Na\,(g) \qquad \text{or} \qquad \tfrac{1}{2}\,Cl_2\,(g) \quad \rightarrow \quad Cl\,(g)$$

Enthalpy change of lattice formation: This is the enthalpy change that occurs when one mole of an ionic compound is formed from ions of the elements in the gas phase. For example:

$$Na^+\,(g) + Cl^-\,(g) \quad \rightarrow \quad NaCl\,(s) \quad \text{or} \quad Ca^{2+}\,(g) + 2Cl^-\,(g) \quad \rightarrow \quad CaCl_2\,(s)$$

Enthalpy change of lattice breaking: This is the reverse of lattice formation – it is the enthalpy change that occurs when one mole of an ionic compound is broken up into ions of the elements in the gas phase. For example:

$$NaCl\,(s) \quad \rightarrow \quad Na^+\,(g) + Cl^-\,(g) \quad \text{or} \quad CaCl_2\,(s) \quad \rightarrow \quad Ca^{2+}\,(g) + 2Cl^-\,(g)$$

Enthalpy change of hydration: This is the enthalpy change that occurs when one mole of ions is surrounded by water molecules to make a solution. For example:

$$Na^+\,(g) + aq \quad \rightarrow \quad Na^+\,(aq) \quad \text{or} \quad Ca^{2+}\,(g) + aq \quad \rightarrow \quad Ca^{2+}\,(aq)$$

Enthalpy change of solution: This is the enthalpy change that occurs when one mole of an ionic compound dissolves in water to form a solution. For example:

$$NaCl\,(s) + aq \quad \rightarrow \quad NaCl\,(aq) \quad \text{or} \quad CaCl_2\,(s) + aq \quad \rightarrow \quad CaCl_2\,(aq)$$

Relationship between enthalpy changes

You used Hess's law during a previous module, and this states that when a change can occur by two different routes, the energy change for each is the same.

$$\Delta H = \Delta H_1 + \Delta H_2 + \Delta H_3$$

Grade boost

Remember that the exam paper will include some questions that cover work from other A-level papers. In this topic you could be asked to use Hess's law; enthalpy changes of combustion and formation and bond enthalpies.

Pointer

At A-level you can treat enthalpy as if it was exactly the same as energy.

Pointer

For a diatomic gas, such as Cl_2 or O_2 the enthalpy change of atomisation is equal to half the bond energy.

Grade boost

The solubility of a compound depends mainly on the enthalpy of hydration being exothermic. This means the enthalpy of hydration for the ions must be greater than the enthalpy of lattice breaking.

Grade boost

If you are given a calculation with balancing numbers in the chemical equation, these must be transferred to the calculation.

Pointer

You may be asked to use enthalpy values (ΔH) or standard enthalpy values ($\Delta H^{\ominus}$). Standard enthalpy values occur under standard conditions of 298 K and 1 atmosphere.

Formation of ionic compounds

The enthalpy change of formation for an ionic compound measures the enthalpy change when a compound is formed from its elements. We can build an energy cycle using the values for individual steps to calculate an unknown value in this process, usually the enthalpy of lattice formation as this cannot be measured directly.

To build an energy cycle to calculate the enthalpy of a change, write the equation that you wish to calculate and then produce an alternative route for the same change.

Example:

$$Na\ (s)\ +\ \tfrac{1}{2}\ Cl_2\ (g)\ \rightarrow\ NaCl\ (s)$$

Equation	Enthalpy value / kJ mol⁻¹
$Na\ (g)\ \rightarrow\ Na^+\ (g)\ +\ e$	496
$Cl\ (g)\ +\ e\ \rightarrow\ Cl^-\ (g)$	−349
$Na\ (s)\ \rightarrow\ Na\ (g)$	108
$Cl_2\ (g)\ \rightarrow\ 2\ Cl\ (g)$	242
$Na^+\ (g)\ +\ Cl^-\ (g)\ \rightarrow\ NaCl\ (s)$	−788

If we are to build a cycle based on the overall equation, then we must find equations in the table that contain the same substances as we have in the overall equation.

We see that we now need to connect the Na with the Na^+ and the Cl with the Cl^-.

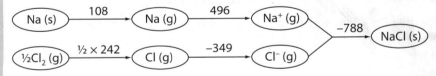

This creates a complete cycle, and we can calculate the overall value by starting at the Na (s) + ½ Cl₂ (g) and then following the cycle around to the NaCl (s).

$$\Delta H = 108\ +\ (\tfrac{1}{2} \times 242)\ +\ 496\ -349\ -\ 788 = -412\ kJ\ mol^{-1}$$

Stability of compounds

One way of judging if a compound is stable is to use the enthalpy of formation. In general, a compound is stable if the enthalpy of formation is negative (exothermic). The more negative the value, the more stable the compound.

Entropy

Entropy is a quantity which measures the freedom of molecules, or atoms within a molecule. Where molecules have greater freedom, this leads to greater disorder. In any natural change, overall entropy will tend to increase.

The molecules in gases have more freedom than those in liquids, with the freedom of molecules in solids being the least. This means that the entropy of a gas will be greatest, followed by liquids, with solids having the lowest entropy. We can write this as:

$$S \text{ (gas)} > S \text{ (liquid)} > S \text{ (solid)}$$

Unlike enthalpy terms, entropy values and entropy changes are given in $J\ K^{-1}\ mol^{-1}$. To calculate the entropy change during a chemical reaction, you can use the entropy of each of the reactants and products. For the formation of water from its elements:

$$H_2 \text{ (g)} + \tfrac{1}{2} O_2 \text{ (g)} \rightarrow H_2O \text{ (l)}$$

$$\Delta S = S(H_2O(l)) - S(H_2(g)) - \tfrac{1}{2}S(O_2(g)) = 70 - 131 - \tfrac{1}{2} \times 205$$
$$= -163.5\ J\ K^{-1}\ mol^{-1}$$

Gibbs free energy

The reaction of hydrogen and oxygen gases to give water has a negative entropy change, but as entropy always tends to increase in natural changes you may think this means the reaction will not happen. The reality is that the reaction between hydrogen and oxygen is very feasible. This is because an exothermic reaction increases the entropy of the surroundings, and we need to factor this into the calculations. The value which combines enthalpy and entropy is the Gibbs free energy, ΔG:

$$\Delta G = \Delta H - T\Delta S$$

If the value of ΔG is negative, the reaction can occur spontaneously.

If the value of ΔG is positive, the reaction cannot occur spontaneously.

This balance between enthalpy and entropy will allow endothermic processes to occur such as boiling, dissolving sodium chloride or thermal decomposition reactions. In each case the greater freedom of the particles in the liquid solution or gas phase causes a significant increase in entropy in the change, and this is greater than the enthalpy change, especially at higher temperatures making the overall value negative.

≫ Pointer

Take care with using S and ΔS. The entropy of a gas would be S (gas) while ΔS refers to the entropy change during a chemical reaction or physical change.

≫ Grade boost

A common error is to use the incorrect units in calculating ΔG. The entropy must be divided by 1000 to convert J into kJ, and the temperature must be given in Kelvin.

 quickfire

⑱ Calculate the entropy change for the reaction below:

$$Na_2CO_3(s) \rightarrow Na_2O(s) + CO_2(g)$$

	Entropy, S / $J\ K^{-1}\ mol^{-1}$
Na_2CO_3 (s)	136
Na_2O (s)	73
CO_2 (g)	214

quickfire

⑲ Calculate the enthalpy change for the reaction above using the enthalpies of formation below.

	ΔH_f / $kJ\ mol^{-1}$
Na_2CO_3 (s)	−1131
Na_2O (s)	−416
CO_2 (g)	−394

Grade boost

QUICKFIRE

⑳ Use the answers to Quickfire questions 18 and 19 to calculate the Gibbs free energy change for this reaction at 300 K.

QUICKFIRE

㉑ Use the answers to Quickfire questions 18 and 19 to calculate the minimum temperature for the reaction to occur.

Using Gibbs free energy

The Gibbs free energy can be used to find out the temperature required for a reaction to occur. As the temperature changes, the value of the Gibbs free energy changes with it due to the inclusion of temperature in the expression:

$$\Delta G = \Delta H - T\Delta S$$

The value of the Gibbs free energy needs to be negative for a reaction to occur, and at the temperature that the reaction just begins to be possible, the value of the Gibbs free energy must just become negative. At this point $\Delta G = 0$, and so you can write:

$$\Delta H - T\Delta S = 0 \qquad \text{so} \quad T = \Delta H \div \Delta S$$

ΔH and ΔS need the same energy units, but are usually given in different ones, so the first step is to multiply ΔH by 1000 to convert it into $J\ mol^{-1}$. The calculation produces a temperature in K.

Example

Calcium carbonate decomposes when heated to form calcium oxide and carbon dioxide:

$$CaCO_3\ (s) \quad \rightarrow \quad CaO\ (s) \ + \ CO_2\ (g)$$

For this reaction $\Delta H = 178\ kJ\ mol^{-1}$ and $\Delta S = 161\ J\ K^{-1}\ mol^{-1}$. Use these values to find the minimum temperature needed for the decomposition to occur.

Answer

At the minimum temperature for the reaction, $\Delta G = 0$ and from this we can show that: $T = \Delta H \div \Delta S$ so that $T = 178{,}000 \div 161 = 1106\ K$.

General equilibria

General equilibria

An equilibrium is set up when a reversible reaction reaches a point where the amounts of reactants and products stay the same because the rates of the forward and reverse reactions are equal. In module CH1 you studied how these amounts changed when temperature and pressure changed, using Le Chatelier's principle. This method does not allow you to work out the amounts of each reactant and product, and to do this you need to use an equilibrium constant.

> **» Pointer**
> Remember that in any equilibrium constant the expression has **products over reactants**.

Writing equilibrium constants

There are two types of general equilibrium constant K_c and K_p. K_c is the equilibrium constant in terms of concentration. It is used for solutions, but can also be used for other types of mixture if you are given concentrations. For a reversible reaction in solution of the type:

$$a \, A \, (aq) \; + \; b \, B \, (aq) \; \rightleftharpoons \; x \, X \, (aq) \; + \; y \, Y \, (aq)$$

The equilibrium constant for the reaction in solution is:

$$K_c = \frac{[X]^x [Y]^y}{[A]^a [B]^b} \quad \text{where [X] represents the concentration of X}$$

The top line has the concentrations of all the products to the powers of the balancing number, multiplied together. The bottom line has the concentrations of all the reactants to the powers of the balancing number, multiplied together. For example:

For the reaction: $Sn^{4+} \; + \; 2 \, Fe^{2+} \rightleftharpoons 2 \, Fe^{3+} \; + \; Sn^{2+}$

The equilibrium constant, K_c, is given by: $K_c = \dfrac{[Fe^{3+}]^2 \, [Sn^{2+}]}{[Sn^{4+}] \, [Fe^{2+}]^2}$

K_p is the equilibrium constant in terms of partial pressures and it is only useful for gas mixtures. We write the expression for the equilibrium constant K_p in a similar way to K_c. For the reversible reaction between gases shown:

$$a \, A \, (g) \; + \; b \, B \, (g) \; \rightleftharpoons \; x \, X \, (g) \; + \; y \, Y \, (g)$$

The equilibrium constant for the reaction is:

$$K_p = \frac{p_X{}^x \, p_Y{}^y}{p_A{}^a \, p_B{}^b} \quad \text{where } p_X \text{ represents the partial pressure of X}$$

The top line has the partial pressures of all the products to the powers of their balancing numbers, multiplied together. The bottom line has the partial pressures of all the reactants to the powers of their balancing numbers, multiplied together. For example:

For the reaction: $N_2O_4 \, (g) \; \rightleftharpoons \; 2 \, NO_2 \, (g)$

The equilibrium constant, K_p is given by: $K_p = \dfrac{P_{NO_2}^2}{P_{N_2O_4}}$

⊙》《《《 quickfire

㉒ Write the equilibrium constant, K_p, for the equilibrium below:

$$4 \, NH_3(g) \; + \; 5 \, O_2(g) \; \rightleftharpoons \; 4 \, NO(g) \; + \; 6 \, H_2O(g)$$

> **» Pointer**
> If you write square brackets in any expression, these mean concentration. If any square brackets appear anywhere in a K_p expression it is immediately wrong.

≫ *Pointer*

Some equilibrium constants have units and some do not. If there are the same numbers of concentration terms on the top and bottom lines of the equilibrium constant then these units cancel out and there are no units. If there are different numbers of concentration terms on the top and bottom lines of the equilibrium constant then some units cancel out, but some units remain behind.

$$\frac{\text{mol dm}^{-3} \times \cancel{\text{mol dm}^{-3}}}{\cancel{\text{mol dm}^{-3}}}$$

Calculating K_p or K_c

You can calculate the values of K_c and K_p if you are given information about the concentrations of reactants and products at equilibrium (for K_c) or the partial pressures of these (for K_p). In a relatively straightforward example, you would be given all the concentrations that you need.

Example: In a mixture of hydrogen and iodine vapours, the following reversible reaction occurs: $H_2 + I_2 \rightleftharpoons 2 HI$

The equilibrium mixture produced during this reaction contains 0.0035 mol dm^{-3} of each reactant and 0.0235 mol dm^{-3} HI. Calculate the value of K_c.

Answer: $K_c = \dfrac{[HI]^2}{[H_2][I_2]} = \dfrac{0.0235^2}{0.0035 \times 0.0035} = 45.1$

Because there are two concentrations on the top line of the expression and two on the bottom, they cancel out and K_c **has no units**.

Working out equilibrium mixtures

If the information given does not list the concentrations of every reactant and product at equilibrium, then you need to work these out. A common example is when you are given the concentrations of each reactant at the start and then given the concentration of **one** product at equilibrium.

Example: If an equimolar solution of A and B where the concentration of each is 0.5 mol dm^{-3} is allowed to reach equilibrium then the equilibrium mixture contains 0.2 mol dm^{-3} of D. Calculate the value of K_c.

$$A + B \rightarrow 2C + D$$

Answer:

	[A]	[B]	[C]	[D]
Concentrations at the start/mol dm^{-3}	0.5	0.5	0	0
Concentrations at equilibrium/mol dm^{-3}	0.3	0.3	0.4	0.2

At the start we only have A and B, both with concentration 0.5 mol dm^{-3}.

At equilibrium we have [D] = 0.2 mol dm^{-3}, but since 2 C are made when each D is made then [C] = 0.4 mol dm^{-3}.

To make 0.2 D we must use up 0.2 A and 0.2 B, leaving 0.3 of each behind.

We now must write an expression for K_c and put these values into it to get the value of K_c. Remember to include the units.

So the equilibrium constant is: $K_c = \dfrac{[C]^2[D]}{[A][B]} = \dfrac{0.4^2 \times 0.2}{0.3 \times 0.3} = 0.365$ mol dm^{-3}

What do equilibrium constants tell us?

Equilibrium constants can give us a guide to the degree that an equilibrium lies towards products or starting materials. An equilibrium that has similar amounts of starting materials and products would have a K_c value around 1.

If K_c is a lot less than 1, then very little of the products are formed, and most of the mixture is starting materials. This is the case when ΔG is positive, as the reaction doesn't occur spontaneously.

If K_c is a lot more than 1, then most of the reactants have been converted into products. This is the case when ΔG for the reaction is negative, as the reaction will occur spontaneously.

Effect of conditions on K_c and K_p

The name 'equilibrium constant' suggests that the values of K_c and K_p would always be the same, and this is generally true. The only factor that will change the value of K_c or K_p is temperature – if we change pressure, add a catalyst or make any other changes, the values of K_c and K_p stay the same. When we change the temperature, we must use Le Chatelier's principle to work out the effect on the equilibrium position.

If the reaction is exothermic, increasing the temperature will shift the equilibrium to the left as this is the endothermic direction. This decreases the products (the top line of the equilibrium constant) and increases the reactants (the bottom line of the equilibrium constant) which makes the equilibrium constant smaller.

If the reaction is endothermic, increasing the temperature will shift the equilibrium to the right as this is the endothermic direction. This increases the products (the top line of the equilibrium constant) and decreases the reactants (the bottom line of the equilibrium constant) which makes the equilibrium constant larger.

Example

$N_2 + 3H_2 \rightleftharpoons 2NH_3$ *Exothermic*

If the temperature is increased, the equilibrium will shift to the endothermic direction, which is to the left, to counteract the temperature change. This increases the concentration of N_2 and H_2 and decreases the concentration of NH_3. The equilibrium constant, K_c is:

$$K_c = \frac{[NH_3]^2}{[N_2][H_2]^3}$$

The effect on this change is to decrease $[NH_3]$ and increase $[N_2]$ and $[H_2]$ which will decrease the value of K_c.

» *Pointer*

When an equilibrium is described as exothermic, this means it is exothermic as it is written. The forward reaction is exothermic and the reverse reaction will be endothermic.

⊙≪≪≪ quickfire

㉓ Explain the effect of increasing temperature on the equilibrium constant, K_p, for the exothermic reaction below.

$2SO_2(g) + O_2(g) \rightleftharpoons 2SO_3(g)$

>> Pointer

You should be prepared to interpret data on different conditions or routes to form a compound. In addition to rates of reaction and yield of products, you should consider aspects of green chemistry. These include the atom economy, whether the starting materials are sustainable and whether any of the side products are harmful.

Equilibria and rates

Equilibrium and kinetic data can both give us information about chemical reactions; however, they tell us different things:

Equilibrium data tells us about the relative stability of the reactants and products, and the energy changes that occur. It tells us nothing about how the reaction occurs.

Reaction rates give us information about the changes that occur between the reactants and transition state. This allows us to deduce what is happening *during* the reaction, giving the **reaction mechanism**.

Applying equilibrium and rate equations

Companies consider kinetic, energetic and equilibrium data when planning any process and any industrial reaction aims to produce the maximum amount of product as quickly as possible using the least energy. Often a compromise is needed which gets each of these as close to each ideal value as possible.

Equilibrium: The equilibrium yield of product can be changed by altering concentration, pressure or temperature. The equilibrium constant tells us which concentration or pressure values favour high yield, and the energetics shows us whether the reaction is exothermic or endothermic.

Rates: The rates can be made as fast as possible by increasing temperature, increasing pressure or adding a catalyst.

Energetics: Energy calculations will identify how much energy needs to be input into the system for a reaction to occur, avoiding the input of excess energy. Similarly, if a reaction is exothermic, we may harness the energy released rather than just lose it as waste heat.

Acid-base equilibria

Acids and bases

In your earlier work you will have seen that Lowry and Brönsted defined **acids** and **bases** in terms of winning and losing H^+ ions and that acids can be classified as strong or weak.

Strong acids donate all of their H^+ ions in aqueous solution, for example hydrochloric acid:

$$HCl\ (aq)\ +\ H_2O\ (l)\ \longrightarrow\ H_3O^+\ (aq)\ +\ Cl^-\ (aq)$$

Weak acids donate some of their H^+ ions in aqueous solution because they set up a dynamic equilibrium, for example ethanoic acid:

$$CH_3COOH\ (aq)\ +\ H_2O\ (l)\ \rightleftharpoons\ CH_3COO^-\ (aq)\ +\ H_3O^+\ (aq)$$

In both of these equations H_2O is accepting a proton and so it is acting as a base, but this is not the only base in each equation. Because the second equation is an equilibrium we can write the equation in either direction, and in the reverse reaction CH_3COO^- accepts a H^+ ion from H_3O^+ – the CH_3COO^- is acting as a base. We call the CH_3COO^- the conjugate base of CH_3COOH, and H_3O^+ is the conjugate acid of H_2O.

pH and acidity

The strengths of acids are usually quoted on the pH scale. This commonly ranges from 0 (strong acid) through 7 (neutral) to 14 (strong alkali).

0	1	2	3	4	5	6	7	8	9	10	11	12	13	14
Strong Acid			**Weak Acid**				**Neutral**			**Weak Alkali**			**Strong Alkali**	

Acids have pH values below 7.   *Alkalis have pH values above 7.*

The further a solution's pH value is below neutral (7), the stronger the acid.

The further a solution's pH value is above neutral (7), the stronger the alkali.

The numbers on the pH scale are calculated from the concentration of $H^+(aq)$ ions in the solution. pH is defined as:

$$pH = -\log_{10}[H^+(aq)]$$

So for a H^+ concentration of 0.15 mol dm^{-3}, pH $= -\log(0.15) = 0.82$.

You can also use this formula to work out the concentration of H^+ in a solution where you know the pH. The rearranged formula is:

$$[H^+(aq)] = 10^{-pH}$$

Since pH is a log scale, one unit is equivalent to a 10 times change in H^+ concentration, so 2 pH units are 100 times and 3 represent 1000 times.

Key terms

Acid = H^+ ion donor (a proton donor).

Base = H^+ ion acceptor (a proton acceptor).

➤➤ *Pointer*

You will see the term proton used interchangeably with H^+, because a hydrogen ion is just a single proton.

Grade boost

Don't confuse strong acids with concentrated acids. Strong and weak refer to how many of the molecules release H^+ ions, while concentrated and dilute refers to how much acid has been dissolved in a volume of water.

quickfire

㉔ Calculate the pH of a solution where $[H^+]$ is 0.015 mol dm^{-3}.

➤➤ *Pointer*

To calculate 10^{-pH} on many calculators you use the INV or SHIFT button before pressing $\log_{10}$.

quickfire

㉕ Calculate the concentration of H^+ in a solution with a pH of 3.2.

≫ *Pointer*

Because all K_a expressions are similar, with two concentrations on the top and one on the bottom, the units are always the same: $mol\ dm^{-3}$.

⊙≪≪≪ quicĸꜰɪre

㉖ Work out the pH of a solution of a 0.5 mol dm⁻³ methanoic acid, HCOOH (K_a = 1.6 × 10⁻⁵ mol dm⁻³).

⊙≪≪≪ quicĸꜰɪre

㉗ A 0.5 mol dm⁻³ solution of a monobasic acid has a pH of 4.5. Calculate the value of K_a for this acid.

Equilibrium constants for acids

The dissociation of an acid is an equilibrium process so it has an equilibrium constant. The equilibrium is:

$$HA\ (aq) \rightleftharpoons H^+(aq)\ +\ A^-(aq)$$

This equilibrium is simplified because it ignores the involvement of water and it has a special equilibrium constant called K_a. For the acid HA:

$$K_a = \frac{[H^+][A^-]}{[HA]}$$

The more dissociated the acid is, the more hydrogen ions and anions there will be, so the larger the value of K_a. A weak acid has a low value of K_a and a strong acid has a high value of K_a.

Calculating pH for strong and weak acids

To calculate the pH of an acid we need to know the concentration of H⁺ ions in the solution. We calculate [H⁺] in different ways for strong acids and weak acids.

Strong acids

For a strong acid, all the molecules of the acid release H⁺ ions so [H⁺] equals the concentration of the strong acid. For example, 0.10 mol dm⁻³ HCl solution would have [H⁺] = 0.10 mol dm⁻³.

$$pH = -\log_{10}[H^+(aq)] = -\log_{10}(0.10) \quad so\ pH = 1$$

Weak acids

For a weak acid, not all the molecules of the acid release H⁺ ions so the concentration of the H⁺ in solution will be less than the concentration of the acid, and will vary from acid to acid. To work out [H⁺] we need to know the value of K_a for the acid. For ethanoic acid, K_a = 1.7 × 10⁻⁵ mol dm⁻³, so to find [H⁺] in a 1 mol dm⁻³ solution we see that:

$$K_a = \frac{[H^+][CH_3COO^-]}{[CH_3COOH]}$$

Since each CH_3COOH molecule that dissociates produces one CH_3COO^- and one H⁺, then [H⁺] = [CH₃COOH] giving:

$$K_a = \frac{[H^+]^2}{[CH_3COOH]}$$

For a weak acid, very few of the molecules have dissociated so we can assume that the concentration of CH_3COOH present is the same as the concentration we put in. In this case this gives:

$K_a = \dfrac{[H^+]^2}{[CH_3COOH]}$ which rearranges to give $H^+ = \sqrt[2]{K_a \times [CH_3COOH]}$

In this example $[H^+] = \sqrt[2]{1.7 \times 10^{-5} \times 1} = 4.1 \times 10^{-3}\ mol\ dm^{-3}$

Using $pH = -\log[H^+] = -\log(4.1 \times 10^{-3}) =$ **pH = 2.4**

Dissociation of water

Although we always write water as H_2O, any sample of pure water will always include a very small amount of H^+ and OH^- ions. This is due to a reversible reaction which is present in all samples of water:

$$H_2O \, (l) \rightleftharpoons H^+(aq) \ + \ OH^-(aq)$$

The equilibrium lies mainly to the right-hand side, so almost all the water exists as water molecules, with a very small amount of ions. Because the concentration of water stays effectively constant, we can write an equilibrium constant called the *ionic product of water*, K_w.

$$K_w = [H^+][OH^-]$$

The value of K_w is constant at a particular temperature, and at 25°C the value of K_w is approximately $1.0 \times 10^{-14} \ mol^2 \, dm^{-6}$.

When an acid reacts with a base, the reaction is the reverse of the equilibrium above and the equation for the neutralisation reaction is:

$$H^+ \, (aq) \ + \ OH^- \, (aq) \ \rightarrow \ H_2O \, (l)$$

>> **Pointer**

Because the expression for K_w is always the same, with two concentrations multiplied together the units are always the same: $mol^2 \, dm^{-6}$.

>> **Pointer**

You need to be able to write expressions and units for K_a and K_w. You do not need to recall values for K_a or K_w.

Calculating pH for strong bases

To calculate the pH of any solution we need to know the concentration of H^+ ions in the solution. Even in a solution of a base there will be free H^+ ions, but there will be fewer than are present in water. To find the $[H^+]$ we need to use the expression for K_w:

$$K_w = [H^+][OH^-] \quad so \quad [H^+] = \frac{K_w}{[OH^-]}$$

For a strong base, all the hydroxide ions will be dissociated from the base so $[OH^-]$ will equal the concentration of the base. For a solution of NaOH of concentration $0.2 \ mol \, dm^{-3}$, with $K_w = 1.0 \times 10^{-14} \ mol^2 \, dm^{-6}$ then:

$$[H^+] = \frac{K_w}{[OH^-]} = \frac{1.0 \times 10^{-14}}{0.2} = 5 \times 10^{-14} \ mol \, dm^{-3}$$

Using our expression for pH $= -\log_{10}[H^+] = -\log_{10}(5 \times 10^{-14}) = 13.3$

quickfire

28 Work out the pH of a solution of a $0.3 \ mol \, dm^{-3}$ solution of the strong base, NaOH.

Buffers

Buffers are solutions whose pH stays relatively constant as an acid or alkali is added. The buffer solution maintains a nearly constant pH by removing any added H^+ or OH^-. Typically, a buffer solution is made from a mixture of a weak acid and a salt from the same acid, e.g. CH_3COOH and CH_3COONa. They are used to keep the pH constant when enzymes are stored or used.

Grade boost

When writing the two equations for explaining buffers, you must identify that one is reversible and the other is not.

How do buffers work?

In the buffer solution, the salt dissociates completely:
$$CH_3COONa\ (aq)\ \rightarrow\ CH_3COO^-\ (aq)\ +\ Na^+\ (aq)$$
The acid dissociates partly in a reversible reaction:
$$CH_3COOH\ (aq)\ \rightleftharpoons\ H^+(aq)\ +\ CH_3COO^-(aq)$$
According to Le Chatelier's principle the high concentration of CH_3COO^- released by the salt will force this equilibrium to the left, meaning that very little of the acid will dissociate.

When an acid is added to a buffer, this increases the concentration of H^+ so the reversible reaction will shift to the left, removing the H^+ ions by reaction with CH_3COO^-.

When a base is added to a buffer, this reacts with H^+ ions and decreases their concentration so the reversible reaction will shift to the right, releasing more H^+ ions from the CH_3COOH.

A similar buffer system for maintaining alkaline pH is based on a mixture of ammonium chloride and ammonia solution. In this case the equilibrium which shifts upon addition of acid or base is:
$$NH_4^+\ \rightleftharpoons\ NH_3\ +\ H^+$$

Pointer

When a buffer has equal concentrations of the acid and salt then $[H^+] = K_a$ for the acid.

pH of buffers

To calculate the pH of a buffer solution you need to assume that all the salt dissociates so $[CH_3COO^-] = [CH_3COONa]$, and none of the acid does so $[CH_3COOH]$ equals the concentration of acid used.

$$K_a = \frac{[H^+][CH_3COO^-]}{[CH_3COOH]} \quad so \quad [H^+] = \frac{K_a \times [CH_3COOH]}{[CH_3COO^-]}$$

If we make a buffer from 0.20 mol dm^{-3} CH_3COOH and 0.20 mol dm^{-3} CH_3COONa (K_a for $CH_3COOH = 1.7 \times 10^{-5}$ mol dm^{-3}) to calculate the pH we need to calculate $[H^+]$ then use the equation for pH.

$$[H^+] = \frac{1.7 \times 10^{-5} \times (0.20)}{(0.20)} = 1.7 \times 10^{-5} \text{ mol dm}^{-3}$$

$$pH = -\log_{10}[H^+] = -\log_{10}(1.7 \times 10^{-5}) = 4.8$$

quickfire

㉙ Calculate the pH of a buffer solution that contains 0.10 mol dm^{-3} HCOOH and 0.20 mol dm^{-3} HCOONa. (K_a for HCOOH = 1.6×10^{-5} mol dm^{-3}.)

Acid-base titrations

When an alkali is added to an acid, a neutralisation reaction occurs. This leads to an increase in the pH as the alkali is added; however, the change does not form a straight line graph. The shape of the graph depends on whether the acid and base are strong or weak.

Strong acid-strong base titration curve (HCl with NaOH)

The pH increases slowly until the amount of NaOH added approaches the amount of HCl, when there is a sudden increase. The middle region of the curve is vertical, before it levels off at the end. The midpoint of the vertical region is called the equivalence point, and here the amount of alkali added equals the amount of acid.

Titration curve for addition of 0.1 mol dm⁻³ NaOH to 25cm³ 0.1 mol dm⁻³ HCl.

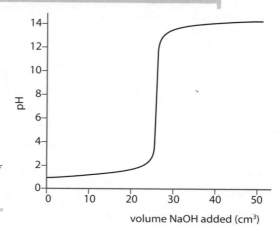

Indicators

We can identify the equivalence point using an indicator. An indicator is a weak acid or base, where the dissociated and undissociated molecules are different colours.

methyl orange (red form)
(in acid)

methyl orange (orange form)
(in alkali)

The indicator changes colour over a small range of pH, but as long as this range lies within the vertical part of the curve then the colour change occurs when only a single drop of the basic solution is added. Different indicators change over different pH ranges, and the values for some indicators are given in the table.

Indicator	Approximate colour change range
Phenolphthalein	8.3 − 10.0
Bromothymol blue	6.0 − 7.5
Litmus	4.0 − 6.5
Methyl orange	3.2 − 4.4

Titration curves including weak acids or weak bases

When a weak acid is used in a titration, the vertical region in the titration curve is shorter, and the curve starts at a higher pH due to the weaker acid. The curve increases more gradually towards the equivalence point, but has a plateau at about half the volume needed for neutralisation. The plateau is due to the formation of a mixture of a salt and acid at this point, and this causes a buffer effect.

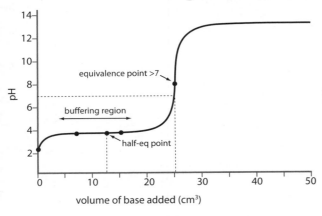

Titration curve for addition of 0.1 mol dm⁻³ NaOH to 0.1 mol dm⁻³ CH₃COOH.

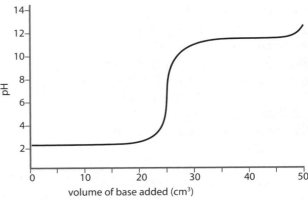

Titration curve for addition of 0.1 mol dm⁻³ NH₃ to 0.1 mol dm⁻³ HCl.

Grade boost

In a weak acid/strong base titration an equimolar mixture of acid and salt is formed when half the volume of base needed for neutralisation is added. This is a buffer and has pH = $-\log K_a$.

Pointer

Since the indicator used in a titration must change colour completely in the vertical region of the curve, not every indicator will work for these titrations. Using the table on the last page we see that phenolphthalein is best for a strong base/weak acid and methyl orange is best for weak base/strong acid.

The strong acid/weak base curve shows a similar pattern in the basic region of the graph, with a gradual increase from pH 7 until it reaches a plateau (buffer effect) and after this it increases gradually to its final pH which will be lower than 14 as the base is weak.

pH of salts

At the equivalence point of each of these curves, we have a solution of the salt formed from the acid and base. The pH of this solution is the mid-point of the vertical part of the curve, and for a strong acid/strong base it is 7 showing that the solution of the salt in this case is neutral. When we have a weak acid and a strong base, the salt formed is not neutral, and it forms a solution that is basic, with a pH of around 8–10. This is because the cation present, e.g. NH_4^+, can dissociate to release H^+ ions in a reversible reaction:

$$NH_4^+ \rightleftharpoons NH_3 + H^+$$

When we have a strong acid and a weak base, the salt formed is acidic, with a pH of around 4–6. This is because the salt releases all its anions, such as the ethanoate anion, CH_3COO^-, and these react and remove H^+ ions from solution due to the equilibrium below:

$$H^+(aq) + CH_3COO^-(aq) \rightleftharpoons CH_3COOH (aq)$$

Summary: CH5 Physical and Inorganic Chemistry

Redox and electrochemistry

Redox reactions

- Any redox reaction has one species being reduced and one being oxidised.
- Oxidation and reduction can be defined using:
  - Electron transfer (oxidation is loss of electrons, reduction is gain of electrons).
  - Oxidation states (during oxidation, oxidation states become more positive, and during reduction they become less positive).

Electrochemistry

- Electrochemical cells are made up of two half-cells joined by a salt bridge and high resistance voltmeter.
- A standard electrode potential is measured by connecting a half-cell to the standard hydrogen electrode.
- Standard conditions are 1 atm pressure, 1 mol dm^{-3} concentration and a temperature of 298 K.
- The EMF of a cell is the difference between the standard electrode potentials of the two half-cells.
- A reaction is feasible if the EMF is positive.

Applications of redox reactions

- Redox titrations give information on concentrations of solutions, using the equation moles = concentration (in mol dm^{-3}) × volume (in dm^3).
- Copper ions can be studied by titration by adding iodide ions, which releases iodine (I_2).
- Fuel cells can be used to obtain energy from fuels.
  - Advantages include high efficiency and no greenhouse gas emissions produced from hydrogen gas.
  - Disadvantages include the use of fossil fuels to produce hydrogen and difficulty of storing flammable hydrogen gas.

p-block chemistry

- Many compounds are amphoteric – they react with both acids and alkalis.
- They can have different oxidation states due to:
  - The inert pair effect – this lowers the oxidation state by 2 and becomes more important down the group.
  - Octet expansion – this allows elements in the third period and below to have oxidation states above +4 by using d-orbitals.

Group 3

- Many compounds are electron deficient – the atoms have fewer than 8 electrons in their outer shell.
- They form co-ordinate bonds with lone pairs, which form dimers such as Al_2Cl_6.
- Boron nitride has a similar structure and bonding to graphite, but it doesn't conduct as the electrons are localised.

Group 4

- They change from non-metals to metals down the group.
- They are stable in the +4 oxidation state, apart from lead which is stable as +2.
- The oxides are acidic at the top of the group, becoming amphoteric at the bottom.
- CCl_4 doesn't react with water, but $SiCl_4$ does.
- Lead(II) compounds are insoluble, apart from $Pb(NO_3)_2$ and $(CH_3COO)_2Pb$.

Group 7

- The elements become weaker oxidising agents down the group.
- The halogens that are stronger oxidising agents can displace the lower halide ions from solution.
- Cl_2 reacts differently with hot and cold NaOH (aq) giving different products in different oxidation states.
- Sulfuric acid reacts with NaCl and NaI, but only NaI is a strong enough reducing agent to reduce the H_2SO_4.

d-block chemistry

- Transition elements lose their *s*-electrons first when they react and have partially filled *d*-orbitals in their ions.
- The elements each have a range of oxidation states.
- They form complexes by bonding with ligands.
- Complexes absorb some frequencies of light, and the reflected light makes them coloured.

Chemical kinetics

- Rates can be measured by studying how any factor (pressure, volume or colour) changes over time.
- The order of reaction gives the effect of each concentration on rate.
- The reaction rate can be calculated from the rate equation, which combines concentrations, orders and rate constant.
- The substances and orders in the rate equation give the rate determining step (slowest step) of a reaction mechanism.

Enthalpy and entropy

- There are many standard enthalpy changes and they all start with or form 1 mole of substance.
- Energy changes can be combined in Born-Haber cycles to work out overall energy changes.
- Stable compounds have negative enthalpies of formation.
- Entropy is a measure of the degrees of freedom in a system, so gases have higher entropy than liquids and solids.
- Gibbs free energy combines enthalpy and entropy, $\Delta G = \Delta H - T\Delta S$.
- For a reaction to be feasible, ΔG must be negative.

Equilibria
General equilibria

- All equilibrium constants have the products divided by the reactants.
- K_p is in terms of pressure, and K_c is in terms of concentration.
- Equilibrium constants often have units which derive from the units of concentration or pressure.
- Equilibrium constants are constant, except when the temperature changes.

Acid-base equilibria

- Acids are proton donors, and bases are proton acceptors, with weak acids dissociating partially and strong acids dissociating fully.
- $pH = -\log [H^+]$, and for a strong acid $[H^+] = [acid]$.
- K_a shows the strength of acids – a larger K_a means a stronger acid, and it can be used to calculate the pH of a weak acid.
- $K_w = [H^+] \times [OH^-]$ and this allows us to calculate the pH of a strong base.
- During acid-base titrations the pH changes unevenly, with different patterns depending on the strength of the acid and base.
- Indicators are weak acids or bases that change colour. An indicator is chosen that changes colour. completely in the vertical region of a titration curve
- Buffers are solutions of weak acids and their salts, which keep pH constant.
- The salt of a weak acid will be basic, and the salt of a weak base will be acidic.

Exam Practice and Technique

Exam practice and skills

Examination questions are written to reflect the assessment objectives as laid out in the specification. Candidates must meet the following assessment objectives in the context of the content detailed in the specification.

Assessment objective AO1:
Knowledge and understanding of science and How Science Works

Candidates should be able to:

- recognise, recall and show understanding of scientific knowledge
- select, organise and communicate relevant information in a variety of forms.

31% of the questions set on the A2 papers are recall of knowledge

Assessment objective AO2:
Application of knowledge and understanding and of How Science Works

Candidates should be able to:

- analyse and evaluate scientific knowledge and processes
- apply scientific knowledge and processes to unfamiliar situations including those related to issues
- assess the validity, reliability and credibility of scientific information.

56% of the questions set on the A2 papers include application of knowledge

Assessment objective AO3:
How Science Works

Candidates should be able to:

- demonstrate and describe ethical, safe and skilful practical techniques and processes, selecting appropriate qualitative and quantitative methods
- make, record and communicate reliable and valid observations and measurements with appropriate precision and accuracy
- analyse, interpret, explain and evaluate the methodology, results and impact of their own and others' experimental and investigative activities in a variety of ways.

13% of the questions set on the A2 papers are on How Science Works

CH4 and CH5: Written paper (1 hour 45 minutes each)

The following is an approximate guide to the structure of the examination papers CH4 and CH5.

Type of question	Marks per question	Number of questions per paper
Structured	10–15	3
Essay	20	2
Total marks		80

The examination questions are written by a principal examiner well in advance of the examination. A committee of experienced teachers and examiners then discuss the paper in detail before approval.

Exam tips

Make sure that you read each question carefully. Under examination pressure, it is all too easy to misinterpret a question and give a sound response that does not answer the question.

Understand the information

At A2 level, around 30% of the questions will be based on knowledge and understanding (AO1). About 60% will be concerned with the application of this knowledge and understanding (AO2). In general the AO2 questions will be more demanding than the AO1 questions. You should consider carefully how you respond, as questions on application will be looking for a more detailed response. The remaining 10% of the questions are concerned with 'How Science Works'. You should read carefully details of your practical work and be prepared to answer questions about laboratory procedures – particularly methods of separation and purification. Other AO3 questions may consider the evaluation of your own and others' work.

Look at the mark allocation

This is an essential part of examination technique. If a question is allocated three marks, then you should be looking to provide three separate points in your answer.

Understand the instructions

Questions begin with key words – these give a clue as to the depth of response that is needed.

State or give

These key words generally need a fairly basic response. Very often these are AO1 questions that are not concerned with any application of known material.

Describe

This generally requires a more detailed response than 'state' and may carry two or more marks. You may be asked to write about a practical procedure or give the structure and bonding of a particular material.

Explain

This will almost always carry at least two marks. It requires a higher level of response than 'state' or 'give' and is often an extension of a 'state or give' question.

Suggest

This key word usually indicates that the answer required is not direct recall and there are a number of possible acceptable answers. A 'suggest' question will require you to think more widely than providing a mere response from the specification. Generally you will be required to use learnt information from the specification and apply it to a new, and unexpected, situation.

Tips about structured questions

Structured questions sometimes require a simple one-word, or one-formula, answer. Other questions will require more detailed answers. You will usually find that the questions in a structural sequence become more difficult as the question theme continues. You should always be prepared to give a diagram in your answer even if the question does not specifically ask you to do this. Sometimes a gap, rather than lines, is left in the question and this is an indication that a diagram may help to illustrate your answer. If there is no 'gap', you should not assume that only writing is required. It may be that the layout of the paper on the page does not allow space for a gap. Any diagrams should always have appropriate labels to help both you and the examiner. Be precise when giving formulae. If a lone pair of electrons is an essential part of your explanation, make sure that you draw these in and they are in the correct position. This is particularly important in questions about shapes and also when describing hydrogen bonding.

Tips about 'essay' style questions

In Chemistry we do not often ask for real 'essay' questions that carry maybe ten marks or more. Since a section B question carries only 20 marks, it could be seen as unfair if half the marks were allocated to a single topic. Instead, longer style questions tend to be split into sections, so that they are in effect, longer structured questions. However, this does not mean that there will be no questions that are worth perhaps six or seven marks. Certain topics lend themselves to more descriptive work. These might include shapes (including structure and bonding), intermolecular bonding, questions about unknown compounds requiring you to use given information including spectroscopic data, transition metal chemistry, and more involved questions on equilibria. In these longer questions you should always check to see if you have given a number of separate points that match the mark allocation. Marks are given for the quality of written communication and you should check that your response is logical, clearly explained with good grammar, and that you have used scientific terms correctly.

Questions and answers

This part of the guide looks at student answers to examination-style questions through the eyes of an examiner. There is a selection of questions on topics in the A2 specification with two sample answers – one of a high grade standard and one of a lower grade standard in each case. The examiner commentary is designed to show you how marks are gained and lost so that you understand what is required in your answers.

Your overall grade will depend on your total marks on the exam. Some questions are more difficult than others so it is important that you work out where you can gain the most marks to get the best grade possible. The examiners will decide how many marks are needed for each grade by studying a selection of exam papers that have gained a particular number of marks, and it is common for these candidates to have gained their marks in different ways depending on the topics they find easiest.

Preparation of alcohols

(a) One method of preparing pentan-3-ol is by the reduction of pentan-3-one.

    (i) State the name of a reducing agent that can be used for this reaction.   *[1]*

    (ii) An infrared spectrum was taken of a sample of pentan-3-ol made in this way. Describe how this could be used to see if any pentan-3-one remained.   *[2]*

    (iii) State how a gas-liquid chromatogram of this sample would show that an impurity was present.   *[1]*

(b) Pentan-3-ol can also be produced by the hydrolysis of 3-pentyl ethanoate, $CH_3COOCH(CH_2CH_3)_2$.

    (i) Give the equation for the hydrolysis of 3-pentyl ethanoate using water as the other reactant.   *[2]*

    (ii) State why aqueous sodium hydroxide is often used instead of water in this reaction.   *[1]*

    (iii) The hydrolysis of pentyl ethanoate involves heterolytic bond fission. State what is meant by the term '**heterolytic bond fission**'.   *[1]*

Tom's answer

(a) (i) Lithium aluminium hydride. ✓ ①

  (ii) If pentan-3-one was present I would see an extra peak at 1750 cm⁻¹. This is due to the C=O bond. ✓✓ ②

  (iii) I would see several peaks. ✗ ③

(b) (i) $CH_3COOCH(CH_2CH_3)_2 + 2H_2O \rightarrow CH_3COOH +$ $(CH_3CH_2)_2CHOH$ ✓ ④

  (ii) It is less dangerous. ✗ ⑤

  (iii) A form of bonding where each atom receives back its own electron ✗ ⑥

Examiner commentary

① Lithium aluminium hydride is an alternative answer.

② Tom has given the correct peak and identified it – two marks.

③ 'Several' peaks means more than two – therefore wrong.

④ Only one mark here as the formulae are correct but the balancing is wrong.

⑤ The use of aqueous sodium hydroxide is actually more hazardous than using water – no mark given.

⑥ Tom has described homolytic fission, rather than heterolytic fission.

Tom achieves 4 marks out of 8.

Seren's answer

(a) (i) Sodium tetrahydridoborate(III). ✓

  (ii) If pentan-3-one was present I would see an extra peak at 1750 cm⁻¹. ✓ ①

  (iii) An extra peak would be seen. ✓ ②

(b) (i) $CH_3COOCH(CH_2CH_3)_2 + H_2O \rightarrow CH_3COOH +$ $(CH_3CH_2)_2CHOH$ ✓✓ ③

  (ii) The hydrolysis of the ester occurs at a faster rate. ✓ ④

  (iii) A process of bond breaking where oppositely charged ions are produced. ✓ ⑤

Examiner commentary

① Seren has only gained one mark as she has not identified the peak at 1750 cm⁻¹

② She has realised that the chromatogram would show an extra peak (due to the impurity).

③ The equation has gained both marks – one for the correct formula and one for it being correctly balanced.

④ The reaction rate is correctly described as increasing.

⑤ She has given an accurate definition of heterolytic fission.

Seren achieves 7 marks out of 8.

Nitromethylbenzenes

(a) The nitration of methylbenzene gives two yellow liquids, 1-methyl–2-nitrobenzene and 1-methyl-4-nitrobenzene. This reaction uses the same nitrating agents as when benzene itself is nitrated.

   (i) State the name of the two reagents used to nitrate methylbenzene. *[1]*

   (ii) The boiling temperatures of the organic reactant and products are:

Compound	Boiling temperature / °C
methylbenzene	111
1-methyl–2-nitrobenzene	225
1-methyl–4-nitrobenzene	238

    Suggest a method that could be used to separate these three liquids from the reaction mixture. *[1]*

   (iii) State the molecular formula of 1-methyl–2-nitrobenzene. *[1]*

(b) (i) 1-methyl-4-nitrobenzene can be oxidised to 4-nitrobenzenecarboxylic acid. State the name of a suitable oxidising agent for this reaction. *[1]*

   (ii) Pure 4-nitrobenzenecarboxylic acid is a solid with a melting temperature of 240°C. State how this melting temperature might change (if at all), if the acid was impure. *[2]*

   (iii) The impure acid contains small traces of compound Y, which produces a silver mirror with Tollens' reagent. The relative molecular mass of Compound Y is 151. Deduce a name for compound Y, giving reasons for your answer. *[4]*

Tom's answer

(a) (i) Nitric acid. ✗ ①

  (ii) Fractional distillation ✓

  (iii) $C_7H_7O_2N$ ✓ ②

(b) (i) No response

  (ii) It would melt at a range of temperatures below 240°C. ✓✓ ③

  (iii)   CHO ✓ ④

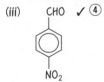

Seren's answer

(a) (i) Nitric and sulfuric acids ✓ ①

  (ii) Distillation ✗ ②

  (iii) $C_7H_7NO_2$ ✓

(b) (i) Alkaline potassium manganate(VII) ✓

  (ii) It would melt at different temperatures and over a range. ✓ ③

  (iii) It must be an aldehyde as it gives a silver mirror. I think that it is 4-nitrobenzaldehyde as this has a molecular formula of $C_7H_5NO_3$ and this has M_r of 151. ✓✓✓ ④

Examiner commentary

① Only one acid has been mentioned.

② A correct order is not necessary

③ Both responses correct

④ Tom has only given the formula of the correct compound. A correct formula is acceptable but there is no reasoning for his answer.

Tom achieves 5 marks out of 10.

Examiner commentary

① Seren has gained the mark as 'concentrated' is not necessary.

② Fractional distillation is required; the compounds could not be separated by simple distillation.

③ Only one mark here – she has not mentioned that the melting temperature would be lower.

④ She has not stated why the compound is 4-nitrobenzaldehyde and has therefore lost a mark.

Seren achieves 7 marks out of 10.

Stereoisomerism

(a) (i) State what is meant by the term **stereoisomerism**. [1]

(ii) *E-Z* isomerism is one form of stereoisomerism. Compound T is the *Z*-form.

$$HOOC,H_3C{-}C{=}C{-}COOH,CH_3$$

Draw the structural formula of the *E*-form. [1]

(iii) Draw the structural formula of an isomer of compound T that is an ester. [1]

(iv) Optical isomerism is another type of stereoisomerism. State what is meant by the term **enantiomer** and describe how enantiomers affect the plane of polarised light. [2]

(v) The formula of compound K, shown below, contains two chiral centres.

$$H-Si-O-Si-C-C-C-H$$

Identify these chiral centres by putting an asterisk (*) on the appropriate atoms. [1]

(b) State the names of reagents A, B and C in the reaction sequence below. [3]

(c) Describe what is observed when 4-bromophenol reacts with aqueous bromine and name the organic product of the reaction. [3]

Tom's answer

(a) (i) Isomerism where the molecular formula is the same but different positions are taken up in space. ✗①

(ii) [structure drawn] ✓

(iii) [structure drawn] ✓

(iv) Isomers that rotate plane polarised light in opposite directions ✓ ②

(v) [structure drawn] ✗③

(b) A → Cl_2 ✗ B → aq KOH ✓ C → conc. H_2SO_4 ✓④

(c) 2,4,6-Tribromophenol ✓ is formed a solid ✗⑤

Examiner commentary

① This answer could be a description of positional isomerism. There is no mention of the same structural formula.

② There is no mention of mirror image forms – only one mark awarded.

③ Tom has only given one correct chiral centre – both are required for the mark.

④ Correct formulae acceptable here. Aqueous potassium hydroxide is ok alternative to sodium hydroxide.

⑤ Tom has not stated the colour of the solid or mentioned decolourisation.

Tom achieves 6 marks out of 12.

Seren's answer

(a) (i) A form of isomerism where the compound has the same structural formula but the atoms take up different positions in space. ✓

(ii)

$$CH_3 \atop CH_3 \Large{\diagdown} \normalsize C=C \Large{\diagup} \normalsize {COOH \atop COOH}$$ ✗ ①

(iii)

$$H_3CO-\overset{\overset{O}{\|}}{C} \Large{\diagdown} \normalsize C=C \Large{\diagup} \normalsize \overset{\overset{O}{\|}}{C}-OCH_3$$ ✓

with H and H below

(iv) Mirror image forms that rotate the plane of polarised light ✓ ②

(v)

$$H-\overset{\overset{H}{|}}{\underset{\underset{H}{|}}{Si}}-O-\overset{*}{\underset{\underset{CH_3}{|}}{Si}}-\overset{\overset{H}{|}}{\underset{\underset{H}{|}}{C}}-\overset{*}{\underset{\underset{H}{|}}{C}}-\overset{\overset{Br}{|}}{\underset{\underset{H}{|}}{C}}-\overset{\overset{H}{|}}{\underset{\underset{H}{|}}{C}}-H$$ ✓

(b) A → HCl ✓ B → aq NaOH ✓ C → conc. sulfuric acid ✓ ③

(c) Bromine water is decolourised ✓ and a white precipitate ✓ of 2,4,6-tribromophenol is produced ✓ ④

Examiner commentary

① The structure is an isomer but is not an *E-Z* isomer.

② Only one mark here as Seren has not stated in which directions the plane of polarised light is rotated.

③ Names are required but correct formulae are acceptable here.

④ All three required points have been given.

Seren achieves 10 marks out of 12.

Nitration

(a) A student was asked to give the mechanism for the nitration of methyl benzenecarboxylate (methyl benzoate). He wrote the following mechanism.

Point out **three** errors in the answer, explaining your answers as appropriate. [4]

(b) Compounds **Q** and **R** are isomers.

compound Q (ring with COOH and CH₃) compound R (ring with COOCH₃)

(i) State the empirical formula of compounds **Q** and **R**. [1]

(ii) State a reagent that will react with compound **Q** but not with compound **R**, giving the result of the test. [2]

Tom's answer

(a) The arrow should go from the electron rich ring ✓ to the electrophile. ✓ ①

(b) (i) $C_8H_8O_2$ ✗ ②

(ii) Sodium carbonate ✓ gas evolved that turns lime water milky. ✓

Examiner commentary

① Tom has gained 2 of the 4 marks. In the intermediate stage the arrow should come from the bond to hydrogen not the bond to the nitro group. He has also not realised that the wrong isomer has been produced.

② The molecular formula has been given rather than the empirical formula.

Tom achieves 4 marks out of 7.

Seren's answer

(a) The arrow should go from the ring towards the NO_2^+. ✓
The ring is electron rich and can act as a nucleophile ✓.
The product given is the 2-isomer but the mechanism
indicates that it should be the 3-isomer. ✓①

(b) (i) C_4H_4O ✓
(ii) Sodium hydrogencarbonate ✓② effervescence will
be seen ✓③.

Examiner commentary

① Seren has gained 3 of the 4 marks but has not realised
that the wrong bond (from the ring to the nitro group)
has been broken in the second stage.

② Both sodium carbonate and sodium
hydrogencarbonate are acceptable answers.

③ 'Effervescence' also gives the result of the test. It is
not necessary to identify the gas as this has not been
requested.

Seren achieves 6 marks out of 7.

Q&A 5

Alcohols and phenol

(a) Complete the table below [4]

Name	Formula	Colour of aqueous solution with Universal Indicator
phenol	C_6H_5OH	
butan–2-ol		green
	$CH_3(CH_2)_3COOH$	

(b) An alcohol **K** is oxidised to a ketone. The mass of 0.20 mole of this ketone is 17.2 g.
(i) Calculate the relative molecular mass of the ketone. [1]
(ii) Deduce a molecular formula for the ketone. [2]
(iii) Deduce a structural formula for the alcohol, explaining your answer. [3]

Tom's answer

(a)

-	-	red ✗①
-	$CH_3CH(OH)CH_3$ ✗②	-
pentanoic acid ✓	-	red ✓

(b) (i) M_r is 86 ✓
(ii) Ketone is R–C(O)–R' M_r of R and R' is 86–28 = 58 ✓
therefore C_4H_{10} ketone is $C_5H_{10}O$ ✓
(iii) Alcohol must be CH(OH) + R + R' ✓③ could be
$CH_3CH_2CH(OH)CH_2CH_2$ ✗④

Examiner commentary

① Phenol is not acidic enough to turn Universal
Indicator to red – there should be a distinction between
the colour given by phenol and a carboxylic acid.

② Tom has given the formula of the wrong alcohol. He
has given propan-2-ol instead of butan-2-ol.

③ This arrangement indicates that a secondary alcohol
is present.

④ The formula is wrong. A CH_2 group is at the end of
the chain instead of a CH_3 group.

Tom has gained 6 marks out 10.

Seren's answer

(a)

-	-	orange ✓
-	$CH_3(CH_2)_2CH_2OH$ ✗①	-
pentanoic acid ✓	-	orange ✗②

(b) (i) $M_r = \dfrac{mass}{moles}$ $M_r = \dfrac{17.2}{0.2} = 86$ ✓
(ii) A ketone is R – C(O) – R' M_r of R and R' is
86 – (12 + 16) = 58 ✓ this is C_4H_{10} ketone $C_5H_{10}O$ ✓
(iii) It must be a secondary alcohol ✓, i.e. – CH(OH) ✓
and could be $CH_3CH_2CH(OH)CH_2CH_3$ ✓③

Examiner commentary

① Seren has given the formula for butan-1-ol not
butan-2-ol.

② An acid will give a red colour with Universal
indicator.

③ There is no requirement to name the alcohol.

Seren has gained 8 marks out of 10.

Q & A 6

(Chloromethyl)benzene

A student makes phenylmethanol, $C_6H_5CH_2OH$, from methylbenzene in two stages.

$$C_6H_5CH_3 \rightarrow C_6H_5CH_2Cl \rightarrow \text{(chloromethyl)benzene } C_6H_5CH_2OH$$

(a) (Chloromethyl)benzene is produced from methylbenzene by reacting it with chlorine, in a radical substitution reaction.

   (i) Write an equation that shows chlorine, Cl_2, undergoing homolytic fission. [1]

   (ii) Calculate the percentage increase in mass of the organic compounds that would occur if 1 mole of methylbenzene is converted to 1 mole of (chloromethyl)benzene. [2]

   (iii) State the name of a reagent that would be used to convert (chloromethyl)benzene to phenylmethanol in the second stage of the reaction. [1]

(b) When (chloromethyl)benzene, M_r 126.5, is made from methylbenzene and chlorine, it can be contaminated with traces of other compounds One of these contaminants contains only C, H and Cl and has an M_r of 161. Suggest a molecular and structural formula for this contaminant and the name and type of mechanism that gives this contaminant. [4]

Tom's answer

(a) (i) $Cl\text{–}Cl \rightarrow Cl^+ + Cl^-$ ✗ ①

   (ii) Increase in M_r 126.5–92 = 33.5 ✗ % increase in mass = 36.4 ✓ ②

   (iii) Sodium hydroxide ✓ ③

(b) 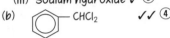 ✓✓ ④

Further radical substitution ✓

Examiner commentary

① The equation wrongly shows heterolytic fission.

② The subtraction has been done incorrectly. However, the percentage has been carried out correctly based on 33.5. A mark has been awarded for 'error carried forward'.

③ The question asks for the name of the reagent – Tom has not stated that aqueous conditions are needed but has been given the benefit of doubt.

④ The correct structural formula has been given. This formula implies that a further chlorine atom is present and therefore this response is worth two marks. However, the molecular formula has not been provided.

Tom achieves 5 marks out of 8.

Seren's answer

(a) (i) $Cl_2 \rightarrow 2Cl\bullet$ ✓

   (ii) 37.5 ✓✓ ①

   (iii) Aqueous sodium hydroxide ✓

(b) The relatively large increase in M_r suggests that another chlorine atom is present. ✓ Formula is $C_7H_6Cl_2$ ✓ Structural formula is:

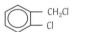 ✗ ②

Examiner commentary

① The question does not ask candidates to show their working. A correct answer gets both marks.

② Ring substitution does not occur under these conditions. Seren has not suggested the name and type of mechanism.

Seren achieves 6 marks out of 8.

Butane-2,3-dione

(a) The diagram shows a blank section of the electromagnetic spectrum.

→ wavelength increasing

  (i) Draw an arrow beneath the diagram to indicate the direction of increasing energy. *[1]*

  (ii) Write 'infrared', 'ultraviolet' and 'visible' in their correct positions on the diagram. *[1]*

(b) In white light butane–2,3-dione is a yellow liquid.

$$H_3C - \overset{\overset{O}{\|}}{C} - \overset{\overset{O}{\|}}{C} - CH_3$$

  (i) State and explain the colour of butane-2,3-dione in blue light. *[2]*

  (ii) Elfed reduces butane-2,3-dione to the colourless liquid butane-2,3-diol. State how he will know when the reaction is complete. *[1]*

  (iii) State one way in which the reduction in (ii) can be speeded up, without the use of increased heat or the use of a catalyst. *[1]*

  (iv) Give the structural formula of any isomer of butane-2,3-dione and state a test that is given by your choice of isomer but not by butane-2,3-dione. Your answer should mention the reagent used and the result of your test. *[3]*

Tom's answer

(a) (i) and (ii)

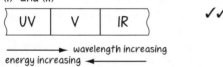

✓✓

→ wavelength increasing
energy increasing ←

(b) (i) It will be blue ✗ as blue light is reflected ✗ ①

  (ii) It will all be clear ✗ ②

  (iii) Heat the mixture ✗ ③

  (iv)

[structural formula drawn] ✓

Tollens' reagent ✓ red precipitate ✗ ④

Examiner commentary

① Blue light is absorbed – no marks here.

② Clear does not have the same meaning as 'turns colourless'.

③ The question stated that heat was not acceptable as an answer.

④ The structure given is correct and will react with Tollens' reagent but this reagent gives a silver mirror, not a red precipitate.

Tom achieves 4 marks out of 9.

Seren's answer

(a) (i) and (ii)

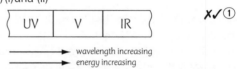

✗✓①

→ wavelength increasing
→ energy increasing

(b) (i) It will appear black ✓ as it absorbs blue light ✓

  (ii) The yellow colour will disappear ✓ ②

  (iii) Make the solution stronger ✓ ③

  (iv)

[structural formula drawn] ✓

Bromine water ✓ becomes clear ✗ ④

Examiner commentary

① Seren has not realised that energy is inversely proportional to frequency.

② 'Disappear' is acceptable but not as good an answer as 'it becomes colourless'.

③ 'Stronger' is satisfactory but not as acceptable as 'more concentrated'.

④ The structure is correct and it will react with bromine water. However, 'clear' means that you can see through it – it is not the same as 'colourless'.

Seren achieves 7 marks out of 9.

Q&A 8

Alcohols and elimination

Propan–1-ol is a primary alcohol.

H−C−C−C−OH with H H H above and H H H below (propan-1-ol structure)

(i) Give the structural formula of two isomers of propan-1-ol. [2]
(ii) State why propan-1-ol does not undergo the triiodomethane (iodoform) reaction. [1]
(iii) Propan-1-ol undergoes an elimination reaction when it is heated with an excess of concentrated sulfuric acid. Give the name of the gaseous organic product and state why this reaction is described as elimination. [2]
(iv) A different organic compound is produced when an excess of propan-1-ol is heated with concentrated sulfuric acid. This product has a relative molecular mass of 102 and contains 15.7% of oxygen by mass, the remainder being carbon and hydrogen. Use the information to suggest a structural formula for this compound, showing all your working. [5]

Tom's answer

(i) [structure: H−C−C−C−H with OH on middle carbon]   [structure: H−C−O−C−C−H]   ✗✓①

(ii) It does not contain the $CH_3CH_2(OH)$– linkage ✗ ②
(iii) Propene ✓ Water is lost ✓
(iv) 15.7 ✗ 102 = 16/100 ✓ therefore 1 oxygen atom ✓
M_r of C_xH_y = 102−16 = 86 ✓ structure must be

[structure: H−C−C−C−O−C−C−C−H heptane-like chain]   ✓ ③

Examiner commentary

① Although this is an isomer of propan-1-ol, the bond to the OH group leads to the hydrogen atom, rather than the oxygen atom. This has therefore been marked wrong.

② The linkage has a $–CH_2(OH)–$ group rather than a $–CH(OH)–$ group.

③ There is a stage missing. Tom has not shown that an 'M_r' of 86 could be C_6H_{14}. This is seen in the answer but candidates have been asked to show all the working.

Tom achieves 7 marks out of 10.

Seren's answer

(i) [structure: H−C−C−C−H with OH on middle carbon]   [structure: H−C−O−C−C−H]   ✓✓

(ii) It does not contain the $CH_3CH(OH)$- linkage ✓
(iii) Propylene ✓① A molecule splitting into two new molecules. ✗ ②
(iv) M_r is 102 and % oxygen is 15.7 If M_r was 100, % oxygen is 16 ✓ therefore only 1 oxygen atom ✓ M_r C_xH_y must be 102−16 = 86 ✓ therefore C_6H_{14} ✓ ③

[structure: H−C−C−C−O−C−C−C−H heptane-like chain]   ✓

Examiner commentary

① Seren has given the traditional name for propene, this is acceptable, as the systematic name has not been requested.

② When describing elimination, it is usual to state that a small molecule (water here) has been removed.

③ This is a very clear and precise answer.

Seren achieves 9 marks out of 10.

Ethanedioic acid

(a) Propylamine reacts with ethanedioyl dichloride, $(COCl)_2$, to give compound G that has the molecular formula $C_8H_{16}N_2O_2$.

    (i) Give the structural formula of compound G. [1]

    (ii) Compound G is hydrolysed using aqueous sodium hydroxide. The mixture is then acidified and the organic product, ethanedioic acid, is obtained by crystallisation. The ethanedioic acid produced is a hydrate, $(COOH)_2 \, xH_2O$, which has a relative molecular mass of 126. Use this information to find the value of x. [2]

(b) Ethanedioic acid can be oxidised by acidified potassium manganate(VII) solution. The equation for this reaction shows that 5 moles of ethanedioic acid react with 2 moles of potassium manganate(VII). In a reaction 0.0102 mole of potassium manganate(VII) reacts with 3.57g of impure hydrated ethanedioic acid, M_r 126. Calculate the percentage purity of the impure ethanedioic acid. [3]

(c) Ethanamide, C_2H_5NO, contains a peptide linkage.

    (i) Write the structural formula of the peptide linkage. [1]

    (ii) Write the structural formula of an isomer of ethanamide that does not contain a peptide linkage. [1]

Tom's answer

(a) (i)

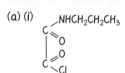

    ✗①

(ii) $(COOH)_2 . xH_2O \rightarrow 126$ M_r of the 'water' = 126−90 = 36

      90   x= 36/2 = 2 ✓✓

(b)   Number of moles of $(COOH)_2.xH_2O$ = 0.0102 × 2.5 = 0.0255 ✓

     Mass of acid = 0.0255 × 126 = 3.21g ✓

     % purity = 3.21/3.57 = 90 ✓②

(c) (i)   ✓

(ii)   ✗③

Seren's answer

(a) (i)

    ✓

(ii) $(COOH)_2 . xH_2O \rightarrow 120$ therefore M_r xH_2O = 120−90 = 30

      90   x = 30/2 = ~2 ✓ ①

(b) Number of moles of $(COOH)_2.xH_2O$ = 0.0102 × 5/2

     = 0.0255 ✓ therefore mass= 0.0255 × 126 = 3.21g ✓

     % purity = 3.21/3.57 = 89.9 ✓

(c) (i)   ✓

(ii)   ✓

Examiner commentary

① Tom has given a structure that does not fit the molecular formula provided.

② The question does not ask for significant figures and so 90 is acceptable.

③ The structure is wrong and shows a three valent oxygen atom, as well as other errors.

Tom achieves 6 marks out of 8.

Examiner commentary

① Seren has wrongly used 120 as the relative molecular mass of the hydrate. The method is correct but a mark has been lost as a result.

Seren achieves 7 marks out of 8.

Q & A

10

Acids and esters

Compounds K, L, M, N and P are all isomers.

compound K   compound L   compound M

compound N   compound P

(i) State, giving a reason, which of these compounds can be hydrolysed to give a carboxylic acid of relative molecular mass 60, as one of the products. [2]

(ii) Compound P can be fully oxidised to a carboxylic acid. State a suitable oxidising agent for this reaction and give the structural formula of the organic product. [2]

(iii) Compound M will produce bubbles of a gas when calcium carbonate is added to its aqueous solution. Explain why this occurs. [3]

(iv) Explain why the boiling temperature of compound K is likely to be higher than the boiling temperature of compound L. You may use a diagram in your answer. A detailed response is not required. [4]

Tom's answer

(i) Compound L as this gives CH_3COOH on hydrolysis. ✗✗ ①

(ii) H^+/MnO_4^- ✓

✓ ②

(iii) Needs to be an acid ✓ these give H_3O^+ ions in solution ✓ ③

(iv) Both compounds have dipole–dipole bonding between molecules ✓ Hydrogen bonding is also present ✓

✗ ④

More energy is needed to break these bonds between molecules ✓

Examiner commentary

① Compound L does not give ethanoic acid on hydrolysis.

② –COOH is acceptable as the structural formula for a carboxylic acid group.

③ There is no mention of the gas being CO_2.

④ The diagram wrongly shows hydrogen bonding between two hydrogen atoms.

Tom achieves 7 marks out of 11.

Seren's answer

(i) Compound N as this gives ethanoic acid, M_r 60, on hydrolysis ✓✓

(ii) Acidified dichromate ✓

✗ ①

(iii) For it to react in this way it must be an acid, giving carbon dioxide ✓✓ ②

(iv) Hydrogen bonding ✓

✓ ③

Examiner commentary

① Seren has not oxidised both the alcohol group and the aldehyde group and therefore given the wrong compound.

② She has missed writing that carboxylic acids produce hydrogen ions, H_3O^+, in aqueous solution.

③ Mention of dipole-dipole bonding is missing and there is no reference to the increased amount of energy needed to separate the molecules.

Seren achieves 7 out of 11 marks.

Diazonium compounds

The red dye, Sudan I, has been used illegally as a food dye. This dye is made by reacting together benzenediazonium chloride and naphthalene-2-ol.

(i) Complete the sentences below, which describe the preparation of benzenediazonium chloride. Benzenediazonium chloride is made by reacting phenylamine with _____ at a temperature of _____ °C. If the reaction temperature rises, the diazonium compound may decompose giving _____ and bubbles of _____ gas.   *[4]*

(ii) Sudan I is then made by adding a solution of naphthalene-2-ol to the prepared solution of benzenediazonium chloride. The mixture needs to be at a pH of ____   *[1]*

(iii) Jessica made some Sudan I by the method above. She found that her yield of the red dye was more than 100%. Suggest two reasons for this yield, apart from errors in calculating the yield.   *[2]*

(iv) When Tom made some Sudan I by the same method he found that his yield was only 57%. Suggest two reasons why errors in his practical work could give this low yield.   *[2]*

Tom's answer

(i) <u>Sodium nitrite / hydrochloric acid</u> ✓① 10°C ✓ <u>phenol</u> ✓ <u>carbon dioxide</u> ✗ ②

(ii) 4 ✗ ③

(iii) Some was lost from the filter paper before weighing ✗✗ ④

(iv) He let the mixture warm up and some decomposition occurred. ✓✗ ⑤

Examiner commentary

① Nitrous acid is made 'in situ' from sodium nitrite and hydrochloric acid, and this answer is acceptable.

② Nitrogen is evolved – carbon dioxide is wrong.

③ The mixture needs to be alkaline not acidic.

④ Only one answer has been given. If some material was lost before weighing, then the yield would have been reduced, not increased.

⑤ Only one answer has been given. The answer to (iii) would have been appropriate here.

Tom achieves 4 marks out of 9.

Seren's answer

(i) <u>Nitrous acid</u> ✓ 5°C ✓ _____ ✗ ① nitrogen ✓

(ii) 7 ✗ ②

(iii) Jessica started with too large a quantity ✓
Her product was still damp ✓

(iv) The temperature was too warm and the diazonium compound decomposed ✓✗③

Examiner commentary

① Seren has not mentioned that phenol is a product when the benzenediazonium compound decomposes on warming.

② Azo dyes, such as Sudan I, are made by treating the diazonium compound with a phenol (or amine) in an alkaline solution. The pH needs to be greater than 7.

③ Only one answer has been given. Another correct response would be that some material was lost during filtration.

Seren achieves 6 marks out of 9.

Q&A

12

Structure determination

An unlabelled bottle containing a colourless liquid L was found in a laboratory store. When it was tested the following information was obtained.

- The mass spectrum showed a molecular ion signal at m/z 116 and a strong signal at m/z 85.
- The empirical formula of the compound was C_3H_6O.
- The infrared spectrum showed a strong signal at 1737 cm^{-1} but there was no broad peak at 2500–3550 cm^{-1}.
- The high resolution NMR spectrum is shown to the right.

Use all the information to suggest a structural formula for Compound L. [9]

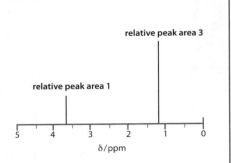

relative peak area 3

relative peak area 1

δ/ppm

Mark scheme

① The molecular ion in the mass spectrum indicates that the M_r of compound L is 116. ② This value means that the formula of compound L must be $(C_3H_6O)_n$. M_r C_3H_6O = 58. n = 116/58 = 2. Molecular formula is $C_6H_{12}O_2$. ③ Since there are two oxygen atoms in a molecule of compound L it must be a carboxylic acid or an ester. ④ The peak at 1737 cm^{-1} in the infrared spectrum indicates that a C=O bond is present. No signal at 2500 – 3550 cm^{-1} indicates that an O-H bond is absent. ⑤ Compound L cannot therefore be a carboxylic acid. It must be an ester, RCOOR'. ⑥ The mass spectrum signal at 85 indicates a loss of 31 from the molecular ion at 116. This is likely to be a methoxy group / –OCH$_3$. *The ester must be a methyl ester / R' is CH$_3$.* ⑦ R must have an 'M_r' of 116 – 59 = 57 (where 57 is the 'M_r' of C=O and OCH$_3$). R must be C_4H_9. ⑧ *The NMR spectrum has two* unsplit signals, which fits with an ester structure as the alkyl groups are not next to each other. The 'butyl' protons must result in the signal at 1.2 δ and contain all equivalent protons. R is $(CH_3)_3C-$. ⑨ Therefore compound L has the structural formula $(CH_3)_3CCOOCH_3$.

Tom's answer

The relative molecular mass is 116 because the molecular ion indicates the M_r value ✓① 'M_r C_3H_6O = 58, therefore formula is $C_6H_{12}O_2$, as 116 is twice 58 ✓② It is an ester as –OH is absent ✓⑤. Fragment of 31 is lost, must be –OCH$_3$, therefore RCOOCH$_3$. ✓⑥ The smaller NMR signal must be the methyl group and therefore the other signal must contain 9 protons, therefore C_4H_9 ✓⑦. Ester must be $C_4H_9COOCH_3$ ✓⑨

Seren's answer

The 'M_r' of C_3H_6O is 58 and since the relative molecular mass is 116, the molecular formula must be $C_6H_{12}O_2$ ✓✓①② Compound L must either be an acid or an ester as there two oxygen atoms present ✓ ③ No O-H peak is present as there is no peak at 2500–3550 cm^{-1} but the peak at 1737 cm^{-1} shows that C=O is present ✓ ④ It must be an ester ✓ ⑤ The unsplit NMR signals are in ratio 3:1 and must be 9 protons and 3 protons, therefore must be C_4H_9 and CH$_3$ ✓ ⑦. All the butyl protons are equivalent (no splitting) ✓ ⑧ The ester must be $CH_3COOC(CH_3)_3$ ✓ ⑨

Examiner commentary

③ No clear explanation has been given for this marking point.

④ There is no identification of the C=O bond.

⑧ Tom has not stated that all the protons are equivalent in the C_4H_9 group.

⑨ The answer for the ester has gained a mark, error carried forward, as the inability to show the structure of the C_4H_9 group has already been penalised.

Summative commentary

Tom's answer is well organised but lacks the information to clearly identify the ester.

Tom achieves 6 marks out of 9.

Examiner commentary

⑥ Seren has not deduced that 'M_r' 31 must be OCH$_3$, therefore a methyl ester.

⑨ She has been given this mark for 'error carried forward' as the wrong ester has already been penalised.

Summative commentary

This is a very good answer but the failure to identify the methoxy group has meant that she has arrived at the wrong ester.

Seren achieves 8 marks out of 9.

Q & A 13

Benzene structure

Benzene was first isolated by Faraday in 1825 from the gas that was being used for lighting. Kekulé suggested that benzene had a six-membered ring structure with an alternating pattern of double and single carbon to carbon bonds. Discuss the currently accepted structure and bonding of benzene, and the evidence that suggests that Kekulé's structure is incorrect. As part of your answer you should comment on why benzene readily undergoes substitution reactions but is resistant to addition.

[8]

Mark scheme

① If the Kekulé formula was correct then it should decolourise bromine water (as addition occurs). ② This decolourisation does not occur. ③ The accepted structure of benzene is that it is a planar molecule with a hexagonal ring of carbon to carbon sigma bonds. ④ In addition the p-electrons of each carbon atom overlap, ⑤ to form a delocalised structure of electrons / π – structure. ⑥ The enthalpy of hydrogenation of benzene is considerably less than the value that should be obtained if benzene had the Kekulé structure. ⑦ Benzene readily undergoes substitution reactions because this maintains the stable electron ring structure. ⑧ In addition, more energy would be needed to 'destroy' the delocalised ring structure.

Tom's answer

Benzene consists of a 6-membered ring of sigma covalent bonds between carbon atoms. ✓③. In addition it has a delocalised system ✓⑤ (a π-system) of overlapping p-electrons ✓④. It undergoes substitution reactions related to the stability of the ring as this retains the more stable ring structure. ✓⑦.

Examiner commentary

① No comment has been made to discredit the Kekulé structure by means of, for example, adding aqueous bromine or potassium manganate(VII) solution. ② There is no comment as to any observations if aqueous bromine or potassium managanate(VII) solution were added.

⑥ There is no reference to the enthalpies of hydrogenation.

⑧ Although reference has been given to the stability of the ring system, Tom has not gone on to write that more energy is required for addition reactions than for substitution reactions.

Summative commentary

Tom has only provided the basic details of the structure of benzene. He has not given any information relating to the stability of the benzene ring.

Tom achieves 4 marks out of 8.

Seren's answer

The C=C double bonds in the Kekulé structure suggest that it should react with aqueous bromine ✗①, this does not occur ✓②. Benzene contains a delocalised ring system of overlapping p-electrons ✓✓④⑤. The enthalpy of hydrogenation is 208 kJ mol⁻¹, less than the 360 kJ mol⁻¹ that would be obtained if benzene had the Kekulé structure. ✓⑥. The delocalised structure of benzene is therefore more stable than the double / single alternating system of carbon-carbon bonds. ✓⑦

Examiner commentary

① Seren has not stated what would be observed if benzene did react with aqueous bromine.

Summative commentary

Seren has given a sound answer but has not fully described the structure of benzene. In addition she has not stated that more energy would be needed if benzene underwent addition reactions rather than substitution reactions.

Seren achieves 5 marks out of 8.

Reduction and oxidation

Acidified potassium dichromate is a common oxidising agent, but adding sodium hydroxide solution causes the reaction below:

$$Cr_2O_7{}^{2-} + 2\ OH^- \rightarrow 2\ CrO_4{}^{2-} + H_2O$$

(i) Give the colour change seen during this reaction. [1]

(ii) Use the oxidation states of chromium to show that this is not a redox reaction. [2]

(iii) The standard electrode potential for acidified potassium dichromate when used as an oxidising agent is +1.33V. Explain what is meant by the term standard electrode potential and describe how this value would be measured. [6]

14

Tom's answer

(i) orange → green ✓①

(ii) The oxidation state of Cr in $Cr_2O_7{}^{2-}$ is +12 and $CrO_4{}^{2-}$ is 2 × +6 = +12.✗ This isn't a redox reaction because the oxidation states don't change. ✓②

(iii) The standard electrode potential is the voltage you would measure if you connected a half-cell to the standard hydrogen electrode (S.H.E.) under standard conditions (1 mol dm⁻³ concentrations, 1 atm pressure for gases and a temperature of 298 ✓✗). The S.H.E. has a platinum electrode dipping in a solution containing H⁺ (aq) ions, with hydrogen gas bubbled over it. ✓③

Seren's answer

(i) It turns yellow. ✗ ①

(ii) Chromium in dichromate = +6; chromium in chromate = +6. ✓ This is not a redox reaction because the oxidation state stays the same. ✓ ②

(iii) The standard electrode potential is the value measured on the high resistance voltmeter when a half-cell is connected to the standard hydrogen electrode.③

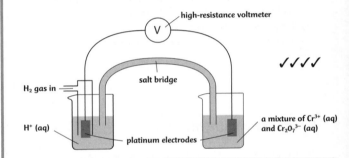

Examiner commentary

① The colour change given occurs when dichromate is reduced, and not in this reaction.

② He has doubled the oxidation state, but has gained a mark for his reasoning.

③ This answer is not precise. He receives marks for giving the substances in the S.H.E. and another for giving two standard conditions. He loses a second mark for conditions by missing the K from 298 K, and loses several marks by not discussing the second half-cell or how they are connected.

Tom achieves 4 marks out of 9.

Examiner commentary

① No mark as the initial colour of the solution is missing.

② Seren gains both marks here.

③ The labelled diagram provides three marks for the substances in each cell, the platinum electrodes. She also gains a mark for the high resistance voltmeter and salt bridge.

She failed to give standard conditions so doesn't gain these marks.

Seren achieves 6 marks out of 9.

Using standard electrode potentials

Dichromate(VI) ions, $Cr_2O_7^{2-}$, react with iron(II) ions in acid solution according to the following equation:

$Cr_2O_7^{2-}(aq) + 14\ H^+(aq) + 6\ Fe^{2+}(aq) \rightarrow 2\ Cr^{3+}(aq) + 7\ H_2O(l) + 6\ Fe^{3+}(aq)$

This reaction can be used as the basis of an electrochemical cell involving the first two of the half reactions shown below:

	E^{θ}/V
$Fe^{3+}(aq) + e^- \rightleftharpoons Fe^{2+}(aq)$	+0.77
$Cr_2O_7^{2-}(aq) + 14\ H^+(aq) + 6e^- \rightleftharpoons 2\ Cr^{3+}(aq) + 7\ H_2O(l)$	+1.33
$S_2O_8^{2-}(aq) + 2e^- \rightleftharpoons 2\ SO_4^{2-}(aq)$	+2.01

(i) Calculate the EMF of the cell. [1]

(ii) Give the cell diagram that represents this cell. [1]

(iii) Identify the reducing agent in the reaction above. Give a reason for your answer. [2]

(iv) Using the standard electrode potentials above, state and explain whether dichromate(VI) ions can oxidise sulfate ions to peroxodisulfate ions, $S_2O_8^{2-}(aq)$. [2]

Tom's answer

(i) EMF = 0.77 – 1.33 = –0.56 V ✗ ①

(ii) $Pt|Cr_2O_7^{2-}|Cr^{3+}||Fe^{2+}|Fe^{3+}|Pt$ ✗ ②

(iii) The iron ion is the reducing agent in this case because it has reduced the chromium from oxidation state +6 to +3. ✓ ③

(iv) The dichromate ions are weaker oxidising agents than the peroxodisulfate ions so they cannot oxidise sulfate ions to peroxodisulfate. ✓ ④

Examiner commentary

① The EMF should be positive, so no mark is awarded.

② Tom does not gain credit here as the ions in solution should be separated by a comma not a line. ($Cr_2O_7^{2-}$, Cr^{3+}, and Fe^{2+}, Fe^{3+})

③ He gains a mark for the reason but 'iron ion' is not specific enough to gain a mark.

④ Tom identifies that the reaction cannot occur and gives a reason so he gains a mark. He does not gain the second mark as the question specifies the use of the standard electrode potentials.

Tom achieves 2 marks out of 6.

Seren's answer

(i) EMF = 1.33 – 0.77 = 0.56 V ✓ ①

(ii) $Pt|Cr_2O_7^{2-}, Cr^{3+}|Fe^{2+}, Fe^{3+}|Pt$ ✗ ②

(iii) The Fe^{2+} is the reducing agent in this case ✓ because it is being oxidised from +2 to +3, and reducing agents are oxidised as they reduce something else. ✓ ③

(iv) The reaction of dichromate ions with sulfate to make peroxodisulfate would have an EMF of:

EMF = $E_{reduction} – E_{oxidation}$ = 1.33 – 2.01 = –0.68 V ✓

A negative EMF means that this reaction is not feasible. ✓ ④

Examiner commentary

① Is correct and gains 1 mark.

② Seren does not gain a mark as she drew the salt bridge as one line.

③ Seren gains 2 marks as she identifies the reducing agent and gives an appropriate reason.

④ Includes a correct identification and reason, and so gains 2 marks.

Seren achieves 5 marks out of 6.

Q&A 16

Redox titration calculations (1)

Iron(II) sulfate exists as a hydrate, $FeSO_4.xH_2O$. A 1.120 g sample of this hydrated compound was dissolved in distilled water and titrated using acidified potassium dichromate(VI) solution, $K_2Cr_2O_7$. This required 27.20 cm^3 of $K_2Cr_2O_7$ solution of concentration 0.020 mol dm^{-3} for complete reaction.

The half-equations for the processes occurring are:

$$Cr_2O_7^{2-} + 14\ H^+ + 6\ e^- \rightarrow 2\ Cr^{3+} + 7\ H_2O$$
$$Fe^{3+} + e^- \rightarrow Fe^{2+}$$

(i) Write an **ionic** equation for the reaction between Fe^{2+} ions and $Cr_2O_7^{2-}$ ions in acid solution. [1]

(ii) Calculate the number of moles of Fe^{2+} ions in the sample of iron(II) sulfate used for titration. [2]

(iii) Calculate the relative molecular mass of anhydrous iron(II) sulfate, $FeSO_4$. [1]

(iv) Calculate mass of iron(II) sulfate, $FeSO_4$, present in the original sample of hydrated iron(II) sulfate, $FeSO_4.xH_2O$ and hence calculate the x, the number of water molecules present in each formula unit of hydrated iron(II) sulfate. [3]

Tom's answer

(i) $Cr_2O_7^{2-} + 14H^+ + 6Fe^{3+} \rightarrow 2Cr^{3+} + 7H_2O + 6Fe^{2+}$ ✗ ①

(ii) Moles $Cr_2O_7^{2-}$ = concentration × volume
= 0.020 × 27.20 ÷ 1000
= 5.44×10^{-4} moles ✓
Moles Fe^{2+} = $5.44 \times 10^{-4} \div 6 = 9.07 \times 10^{-5}$ ✗ ②

(iii) M_r = 55.8 + 32.1 + 16.0 × 4 = 215.9 ✓ ③

(iv) Mass $FeSO_4$ = $5.44 \times 10^{-4} \times 215.9 = 0.117g$ ✗
Mass water = 1.120 − 0.117 = 1.003g ✓
x = 1.003/0.117 = 8.5 ✗ ④

Examiner commentary

① In part (i) he has mixed up Fe^{2+} and Fe^{3+}.

② The moles of dichromate are correct, but he uses the reacting ratio the wrong way around in part (ii).

③ Part (iii) is correct.

④ In part (iv) he uses the wrong number of moles. If he had used 9.07×10^{-5} correctly he would have gained a method mark. He gains a mark for his working in the second step, but the third is wrong.

Tom achieves 3 marks out of 7.

Seren's answer

(i) $Cr_2O_7^{2-} + 14H^+ + 6Fe^{2+} \rightarrow 2Cr^{3+} + 7H_2O + 6Fe^{3+}$ ✓ ①

(ii) Moles $Cr_2O_7^{2}$ = concentration × volume
= 0.020 × 27.20 ÷ 1000
= 5.44×10^{-4} moles ✓
Moles Fe^{2+} = $5.44 \times 10^{-4} \times 6 = 3.26 \times 10^{-3}$ ✓

(iii) M_r = 55.8 + 32.1 + (16.0 × 4) = 215.9 ✓

(iv) Mass $FeSO_4$ = $3.26 \times 10^{-3} \times 215.9 = 0.7g$ ✗ ②
Mass water = 1.120 − 0.7 = 0.4120g ✓
Moles water = 0.4120 ÷ 18.02 = 2.286×10^{-2}
x = moles water ÷ moles $FeSO_4$ =
$2.286 \times 10^{-2} \div 3.26 \times 10^{-3} = 7.01 \approx 7$ ✓

Examiner commentary

① Parts (i) to (iii) are correct.

② Part (iv) needs the mass of $FeSO_4$ and the value of x. The mass of $FeSO_4$ given is 0.7g and this is too few significant figures. Examiners penalise significant figures where the answer is overtruncated, so if in doubt use more figures rather than less.

Seren achieves 6 marks out of 7.

Q&A 17

Redox titration calculations (2)

(i) Cu^{2+} (aq) ions react with iodide ions to produce copper(I) iodide and iodine, I_2, as the only products. Write an equation for this reaction. *[1]*

(ii) The iodine released can be reduced using sodium thiosulfate solution. Show that 1 $S_2O_3^{2-}$ reacts with the iodine produced by 1 Cu^{2+}. *[2]*

(iii) Bronze contains a significant amount of copper. A 0.98g piece of bronze was dissolved in acid and made up to a volume of 250.0 cm^3. Excess potassium iodide was added to a 25.0 cm^3 sample of this solution, and the resulting solution titrated with sodium thiosulfate solution. It took exactly 22.75 cm^3 of sodium thiosulfate solution of concentration 0.0500 mol dm^{-3} to react with the iodine released. Calculate the mass of copper present in the original piece of bronze, and hence calculate the percentage copper by mass in this alloy. *[4]*

Tom's answer

(i) $Cu^{2+} + 4I^- \longrightarrow CuI_2 + I_2$ ✗

(ii) $S_2O_3^{2-} + I_2 \longrightarrow S_2O_3 + 2I^-$
In this equation 1 $S_2O_3^{2-}$ reacts with 1I_2 to make 2I^-. In part (i) 1 copper ion makes 1I_2. These ratios combine to make it 1:1 overall. ✗ ①

(iii) Moles = $0.05 \times 22.75 \div 1000 = 1.1 \times 10^{-3}$ ✓
Moles in 250 cm^3 = $1.1 \times 10^{-3} \times 10 = 1.1 \times 10^{-2}$ ✓
Mass of Cu = $1.1 \times 10^{-2} \times 63.5 = 0.7g$ ✗
Percentage by mass = $0.7 \div 0.98 \times 100 = 74\%$ ✓ ②

Examiner commentary

Tom shows a poor understanding of the concepts behind this redox titration but a good understanding of calculations.
① In both parts (i) and (ii) he has misidentified the products of both reactions, leading to incorrect reacting ratios.
② The calculation is correct, and he gains 3 out of the 4 marks available, and only loses a mark for overtruncation of the mass to 0.7g.

Tom achieves 3 marks out of 7.

Seren's answer

(i) $2Cu^{2+} + 4I^- \longrightarrow 2CuI + I_2$ ✓

(ii) In the equation above $2Cu^{2+} \longrightarrow 1I_2$.
$2S_2O_3^{2-} + I_2 \longrightarrow S_4O_6^{2-} + 2I^-$
In this equation $2S_2O_3^{2-}$ reacts with 1I_2. ✓
Since $2Cu^{2+} = 1I_2$ and $2S_2O_3^{2-} = 1I_2$, so
$2Cu^{2+} = 2S_2O_3^{2-}$ and $1Cu^{2+} = 1S_2O_3^{2-}$ ✓ ①

(iii) Moles $S_2O_3^{2-} = 0.05 \times 22.75 \div 1000 = 1.1375 \times 10^{-3}$ ✓
Moles Cu^{2+} = Moles $S_2O_3^{2-} = 1.1375 \times 10^{-3}$ ✗
Mass of Cu = $1.1375 \times 10^{-3} \times 63.5 = 0.07223g$ ✓
Percentage by mass = $0.072 \div 0.98 \times 100 = 7.37\%$ ✓ ②

Examiner commentary

An excellent answer that gains almost full marks.
① The answers for parts (i) and (ii) gain all the marks available.
② Part (iii) gains 3 out of 4 marks, one for calculating the amount of thiosulfate, and one each for the methods in calculating the mass of copper and the percentage by mass. She loses a mark for failing to realise that the amount of moles she has calculated are in 25 cm^3 and they need to be converted to the moles in 250 cm^3 by multiplying by 10.

Seren achieves 6 marks out of 7.

Q&A

18

p-block elements

This question discusses the chemistry of some element chlorides of formula XCl_3, commonly called trichlorides.

(a) Aluminium chloride, $AlCl_3$, is considered to be an amphoteric compound.

   (i) State what is meant by the term *amphoteric*. [1]

   (ii) Magnesium chloride contains the non-amphoteric element magnesium. Explain how sodium hydroxide can be used to distinguish between solutions of aluminium chloride and magnesium chloride. [3]

(b) Phosphorous and nitrogen can also form trichlorides, PCl_3 and NCl_3, but phosphorous can also form another chloride, PCl_5. Explain why phosphorous can form phosphorous(V) chloride but nitrogen cannot form a similar chloride. [2]

Tom's answer

(a) (i) Amphoteric compounds have acidic or basic properties. ✗ ①

   (ii) Aluminium chloride solution reacts with sodium hydroxide to give a white precipitate but magnesium chloride is basic so it doesn't react with sodium hydroxide. ✗ ②

(b) Phosphorous can form five bonds because it has d-orbitals in the outer shell. This means that it has enough orbitals to hold the five electron pairs, so it can form five covalent bonds using its five electrons. ✓ ③

Examiner commentary

Tom loses many marks for carelessness in his answers.

① It is clear that Tom has some idea but by saying acidic OR basic rather than acidic AND basic the answer is not sufficiently clear.

② Tom gains no marks as he displays a common misconception that amphoteric compounds react with sodium hydroxide but non-amphoteric compounds do not.

③ Tom has a good explanation of why phosphorous can form five bonds but does not explain why nitrogen does not. He gains one mark for this.

Tom achieves 1 mark out of 6.

Seren's answer

(a) (i) Amphoteric compounds react with both acids and bases. ✓ ①

   (ii) Both aluminium chloride and magnesium chloride solutions react with sodium hydroxide to give a white precipitate. ✓ With excess sodium hydroxide, the aluminium hydroxide precipitate dissolves ✓ but the magnesium one doesn't. ✓ ②

(b) Phosphorous can form five bonds because it has d-orbitals in the outer shell, but nitrogen does not have this d-sub shell. To form a bond an atom needs an orbital with one electron, so five orbitals are needed for five bonds. ✓ Nitrogen has 4 orbitals (1s and 3p) so it is limited to a maximum of four covalent bonds ✓, but phosphorous has 9 orbitals (1s, 3p and 5d) so it can form five bonds with its five electrons. ③

Examiner commentary

① Amphoteric defined clearly.

② Her answer contains all key points (the use of excess sodium hydroxide, the white precipitate formed with both solutions, the precipitate with aluminium dissolving in excess but the other not).

③ Covers the reasons for phosphorous forming 5 bonds and nitrogen not forming 5 bonds.

Seren achieves 6 marks out of 6.

Group 3

(a) Aluminium chloride, $AlCl_3$, commonly exists as the dimer Al_2Cl_6.
Draw the structure of the dimer, and explain why the two $AlCl_3$ monomers join together.

[3]

(b) Both boron nitride, BN, and carbon, C, form hexagonal graphite-type structures.
Explain why:
- BN and C can both adopt a hexagonal structure.
- Both BN and C exhibit lubricating properties.
- C is an electrical conductor but BN is an insulator.

[6]

Tom's answer

(a)

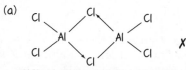

AlCl$_3$ is electron deficient and each chlorine has lone pair of electrons. ✓ ①

(b) Carbon and BN form layers of hexagons with each atom covalently bonded to three others.✓ The layers have weak forces between them, so the layers can move and cause the materials to be soft and act as lubricants. ✓✓
Carbon and BN both have additional electrons and the ones in graphite are delocalised but the ones in BN are not. ✓ This explains why graphite can conduct and BN cannot. ✗ ②

Seren's answer

(a)

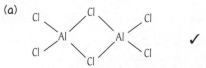

The aluminium atom is electron-deficient. ✓ The chlorine atoms have lone pairs, so they can form co-ordinate bonds with the aluminium. ✓ ①

(b) Carbon in graphite forms layers of hexagons with each carbon covalently bonded to three others. ✓ The fourth electron is delocalised to form a cloud of electrons between the layers. This allows the graphite to conduct electricity as the electrons can move. ✓ In boron nitride, each boron is covalently bonded to three nitrogen atoms. Each nitrogen has a lone pair, and this is localised on each atom and the electrons can't move, so it can't conduct electricity. ✓ The forces between the layers in both are weak so the layers can slip over each other. ✓✓✗ ②

Examiner commentary

① The arrows point in the wrong direction so he gains no mark. The chlorine lone pairs gains a mark but the Al is electron-deficient not the AlCl$_3$.

② Tom has followed the order of the bullet points to try to address every point required, and this is a good idea. He gains 1 mark for the structures, 2 for the explanation of the lubricating properties and 1 for the conductivity. He would need to refer to the electronic structures of both to gain an additional mark on bonding and structure and he would need to discuss how the electrons affect conductivity.

Tom achieves 5 marks out of 9.

Examiner commentary

① An excellent answer gaining all 3 marks.

② Although Seren has not followed the order of the bullet points, she has given a good answer covering each of the marking points. The only point she has not included is the fact that the compounds are isoelectronic, which explains the similarities between them.

Seren achieves 8 marks out of 9.

Q&A

20

Group 4

(a) Iron is usually extracted from iron(III) oxide, Fe_2O_3, in a blast furnace according to the equation below:

$$Fe_2O_3 + 3\ CO \rightarrow 2\ Fe + 3\ CO_2$$

  (i) Explain in terms of oxidation states why carbon monoxide is considered to be the reducing agent in this reaction.   *[2]*

  (ii) Explain why carbon monoxide, CO, can be used as a reducing agent but the corresponding oxide of lead, PbO, cannot.   *[2]*

(b) Describe what is seen when CCl_4 and $SiCl_4$ are added to water separately, giving reasons for any differences.   *[3]*

Tom's answer

(a) (i) The oxidation state of CO is +2 and of CO_2 is +4 ✗. This has gained electrons so it is a reducing agent. ✗ ①

  (ii) Lead is stable in the +2 oxidation state while carbon is stable as a +4 oxidation state ✓. This means that CO will try to convert to CO_2 by reducing something else. ②

(b) When CCl_4 is added to water no reaction happens ✓. When $SiCl_4$ is added to water there are bubbles formed. The difference is because the silicon has d-orbitals. ③

Examiner commentary

① Oxidation states refer to atoms not molecules, so no marks for this. The second part of the answer is totally incorrect.

② A correct statement on oxidation states gains 1 mark, but no explanation so he doesn't gain the second mark.

③ He gains a mark for the observations with CCl_4, but two observations are needed for a mark for $SiCl_4$. The reason given does not compare $SiCl_4$ with CCl_4 so no mark.

Tom achieves 2 marks out of 7.

Seren's answer

(a) (i) In CO carbon has an oxidation state of +2 and in CO_2 it is +4. ✓ Carbon has been oxidised so it must be a reducing agent. ✓ ①

  (ii) Carbon's stable oxidation state is +4. Lead's stable oxidation state is +2 ✓, due to the increase in the inert pair effect on going down the group ✓. This means that PbO is stable and will not want to be oxidised but CO will be oxidised easily. ②

(b) When CCl_4 is added to water it sinks and forms a separate layer ✓. When $SiCl_4$ is added to water, there is an exothermic reaction and bubbles of white fumes of HCl ✓. A white precipitate forms. $SiCl_4$ reacts because it has d-orbitals in its outer shell which water can bond with to start a reaction. Carbon does not have these orbitals so it cannot react. ✓ ③

Examiner commentary

① Oxidation states and explanation gain 2 marks.

② Oxidation states and the inert pair effect gain a further 2 marks.

③ Seren gains 2 marks for the observations, 1 for an observation for CCl_4, and 1 for two observations with $SiCl_4$. The comparison of $SiCl_4$ with CCl_4 clearly gives an explanation for the differences.

Seren achieves 7 marks out of 7.

Q & A

21

Group 7 (1)

Sodium chloride and sodium iodide are both compounds which contain halide ions.

(a) Silver nitrate solution may be used to differentiate between solutions of sodium chloride and sodium iodide. Give the observations that would be expected in both cases. *[1]*

(b) Both sodium chloride and sodium iodide react with concentrated sulfuric acid. The observations made during both reactions are very different. Discuss the reactions occurring. Your answer should include:

- the observations made during both reactions,
- the identities of any products,
- the reasons for any differences in the reactions that occur. *[5]*

Tom's answer

(i) Iodide gives a yellow precipitate and the chloride gives a white precipitate. ✓ ①

(ii) Sodium chloride reacts with sulfuric acid to produce HCl and $NaHSO_4$. We see white, misty fumes. ✓ When sodium iodide reacts with sulfuric acid this produces HI and $NaHSO_4$. We see this as misty fumes as well. The HI reduces the sulfuric acid producing purple fumes of I_2 and a bad egg smell of SO_2. ✓✓ The difference is due to the reducing power of iodine, which is stronger than that of chlorine. ✗ ②

Examiner commentary

① This answer gains the mark.

② The observation for the reaction of NaCl is correct and gains a mark. For the reaction of NaI two observations are required for a mark, and misty fumes and purple fumes gain this mark. The bad egg smell is linked to SO_2 which is incorrect so no credit is given for this. Apart from SO_2 there are three compounds named (HI, HCl, $NaHSO_4$) and this gains 1 mark.

No marks are given for the explanation as he discusses the reducing power of iodine. Iodine is an oxidising agent – iodide is a reducing agent.

Tom achieves 4 marks out of 6.

Seren's answer

(i) Sodium chloride gives a white precipitate, while sodium iodide gives a yellow precipitate. ✓ ①

(ii) When sulfuric acid reacts with sodium chloride it makes HCl and these are released as steamy fumes. ✓ A similar reaction occurs with sodium iodide, releasing HI as steamy fumes. HI is a stronger reducing agent than HCl and can reduce H_2SO_4 to SO_2, S and H_2S ✓✓ while HCl cannot do this ✓. We will see purple fumes and a brown solution and black solid formed. ✓ ②

Examiner commentary

① This answer gains the mark.

② The observation for the reaction of NaCl gains a mark, and the observations with NaI gains a mark for two observations. The observations of purple fumes, brown solution and black solid are all due to iodine so only one of these is allowed. Five different products are identified and this gains 2 marks. The reasons for the differences are explained clearly and gain a mark.

Seren achieves 6 marks out of 6.

Q&A

22

Group 7 (2)

Chlorine reacts with sodium hydroxide in two different ways depending on the conditions used. Discuss the reactions that can occur and the products made. Your answer should show:

- the conditions used for the different reactions,
- the identities of any products, and uses of any chlorine-containing products,
- the equations for any reactions. [7]

Tom's answer

Chlorine reacts with dilute sodium hydroxide solution to do this reaction: ✗
$Cl_2 + 2\,NaOH \rightarrow NaCl + NaOCl + H_2O$ ✓✓①
The NaCl can be used as table salt and the NaOCl can be used as a bleach. ✓
Chlorine reacts with concentrated sodium hydroxide solution in this reaction:
$1\tfrac{1}{2}\,Cl_2 + 4\,NaOH \rightarrow 2\,NaCl + NaClO_3 + 2\,H_2O + Na^+$ ✓✗
The NaCl can be used as table salt and the $NaClO_3$ can be used as a pesticide. ✗②

Seren's answer

When cold, aqueous sodium hydroxide reacts with chlorine it makes NaCl (used as a food preservative) and NaOCl (used as bleach) ✓✓✓. The equation for this is:
$Cl_2 + 2\,NaOH \rightarrow NaCl + NaOCl + H_2O$ ✓①
Chlorine reacts with hot concentrated sodium hydroxide solution to make NaCl and $NaClO_3$ (weedkiller). ✓✓
$Cl_2 + 6\,NaOH \rightarrow 5\,NaCl + NaClO_3 + 3\,H_2O$ ✓②

Examiner commentary

① The conditions given are not sufficient for the mark, as he does not refer to temperature.

For the first reaction, the equation is correct and gains a mark for the equation and a further mark for the products. A third mark is awarded for the correct uses for each product.

② For the second reaction, the equation gives the correct products for a mark but it is not balanced and so no further mark. The use given for $NaClO_3$ is incorrect so no mark is given for this.

Tom achieves 4 marks out of 7.

Examiner commentary

The conditions given for both reactions are enough for a mark.

① For the first reaction, the equation is correct and gains a mark for the equation and a further mark for the products. A third mark is awarded for the correct uses for each product.

② For the second reaction, the equation is correct and gains a mark with a further mark for the products. The use given for $NaClO_3$ is correct, and the use for NaCl has already been given.

Seren achieves 7 marks out of 7.

Q&A 23

Transition metals (1)

(a) Copper(II) ions can form the following coloured complexes: $[Cu(H_2O)_6]^{2+}$ and $[CuCl_4]^{2-}$.
   (i)   State the shape and colour for each complex. [2]
   (ii) Describe the bonding in copper(II) complexes. [2]
   (iii) Explain why the complex $[Cu(H_2O)_6]^{2+}$ is coloured. [3]
(b) Give the electronic configuration of copper(I) ions, Cu^+, and state why copper(I) compounds are not usually coloured. [2]

Tom's answer

(a) (i) $[Cu(H_2O)_6]^{2+}$ = octahedral, royal blue; ✗ $[CuCl_4]^{2-}$ = tetrahedral, yellow. ✓①

(ii) Complexes consist of a Cu^{2+} ion surrounded by small molecules called ligands that are bonded to it. ✓✗②

(iii) The d-orbitals in the transition metal are split into two energy levels, 3 lower and 2 higher. Electrons are promoted from the lower to the higher energy level by absorbing particular colours of light ✓, making the complex coloured. ✗③

(b) The electron configuration of a Cu^+ ion is $1s^2 2s^2 2p^6 3s^2 3p^6 3d^{10}$ ✓. The energy levels are not split so light is not absorbed. ✗④

Examiner commentary

① Tom has the correct shapes and colours except for the colour of the second complex.

② In part (a) (ii) the arrangement of ions and ligands are clear, but the type of bonding present is needed for the second mark.

③ Tom does not give the cause of the d-orbital splitting. He identifies the movement of electrons to higher energy level by absorbing light, but needs to specify that the colour seen is the remaining colours which are not absorbed.

④ He gains a mark for the correct electronic configuration, but the reason is incorrect.

Tom achieves 4 marks out of 9.

Seren's answer

(a) (i) $Cu(H_2O)_6]^{2+}$ = octahedral, pale blue; $[CuCl_4]^{2-}$ = tetrahedral, green. ✓✓

(ii) Complexes consist of a Cu^{2+} ion surrounded by small molecules with lone pairs called ligands that form co-ordinate bonds with it. ✓✓

(iii) When ligands bond to the metal ion, they cause the d-orbitals to split in energy, with 3 lower and 2 higher energy levels. Electrons can move from the lower to the higher level by absorbing the correct amount of energy. This corresponds to a particular frequency of light, which gives the colour of the complex. ✓✓①

(b) The electron configuration of a Cu^+ ion is $1s^2 2s^2 2p^6 3s^2 3p^6 3d^{10}$. The d-orbitals are full, so there is no space for electrons to move, and so no frequencies of light are absorbed. ✓✓②

Examiner commentary

① Seren loses 1 mark in part (a). In part (iii) she has failed to indicate that it is the frequencies of light NOT absorbed that give the colour of the complex.

② In part (b), Seren gains both marks for correctly identifying the electronic configuration and the fact that the d-orbitals are full.

Seren achieves 8 marks out of 9.

Transition metals (2)

(c) Explain why chromium and copper are considered to be transition elements, but zinc is not. [1]

(d) Describe what is seen when excess sodium hydroxide solution is slowly added to a solution of chromium(III) chloride, $CrCl_3$, giving chemical equations for any reactions occurring. [4]

(e) Give a common use for a named transition metal or transition metal compound in industry, and a biological use of a different named transition metal. [2]

Tom's answer

(c) Chromium and copper both have partially filled d-orbitals in at least one of their ions, but zinc forms Zn^{2+} which has a full set of d-orbitals. ✓①

(d) On adding sodium hydroxide solution to chromium(III) chloride solution, a grey-green precipitate forms that redissolves in excess sodium hydroxide solution. ✓

$$Cr^{3+} + 3\ OH^- \longrightarrow Cr(OH)_3 \quad ✓②$$
$$Cr(OH)_3 + OH^- \longrightarrow [Cr(OH)_4]^- \quad ✗③$$

(e) Iron is used as a catalyst for the production of ammonia and is also present in haemoglobin in the blood. ✓✗④

Seren's answer

(c) Chromium and copper both have partially filled d-orbitals but zinc has a full set of d-orbitals. ✓①

(d) Chromium(III) chloride solution is dark green, and when some sodium hydroxide solution is added a grey-green precipitate forms ✓. Adding more sodium hydroxide causes the precipitate to dissolve to form a green solution. that

$$Cr^{3+} + 3\ OH^- \longrightarrow Cr(OH)_3 \quad ✓$$
$$Cr(OH)_3 + 3\ OH^- \longrightarrow [Cr(OH)_6]^{3-} \quad ✓②$$

(e) Copper is used in electronics ✓. Cobalt in present in vitamin B–12. ✓③

Examiner commentary

① Tom gains the mark for part (c).

② He gains two marks for part (d), as he gives one observation (the grey-green precipitate) and one correct equation. It is important to give the observations throughout to gain the full marks, and this includes the colours of the original solution and the final solution (green in both cases).

③ The second equation given is incorrect as three hydroxide ions need to react to form the correct complex.

④ One mark is awarded for a correct use, but Tom has failed to read the question which requires uses of two different metals.

Tom is awarded 4 marks out of 7.

Examiner commentary

① Seren doesn't gain a mark for (c) as she doesn't mention ions but

② She gains full marks for part (d), as she gives descriptions of what is observed before adding sodium hydroxide, with a small amount of the solution added and with excess added. Both equations are also correct.

③ Seren lists uses of two different metals, one in industry and one in biology and so gains both marks for this question.

Seren is awarded 6 marks out of 7.

Q&A

25

Measuring rates of reaction

Nitrogen(V) oxide, N_2O_5, decomposes according to the equation:
$$2\,N_2O_5\,(g) \rightarrow 4\,NO_2\,(g) + O_2\,(g)$$
Colourless   brown   colourless

(a) Suggest two ways of measuring the rate of this reaction. [2]

(b) Under most conditions the rate of this reaction is given by:
$$\text{Rate} = k\,[N_2O_5]$$
When the concentration of N_2O_5 is 4.00×10^{-3} mol dm^{-3} the rate of the reaction was found to be 3.00×10^{-5} mol dm^{-3} s^{-1}.

  (i) Calculate the value of the rate constant to **three** significant figures, giving its units. [3]

  (ii) If the reaction were repeated with an initial concentration of N_2O_5 of 6.00×10^{-3} mol dm^{-3}, calculate the expected value of the rate of reaction. [1]

  (iii) The reaction was repeated at a higher temperature. Explain in terms of collision theory why this will increase the rate of reaction. [3]

Tom's answer

(a) The rate could be measured using colorimetry ✗ or by measuring the amount of NO_2 produced. ✗ ①

(b) (i) k = Rate ÷ $[N_2O_5]$ = 3.00×10^{-3} ÷ 4.00×10^{-5}
= 0.75×10^{-2} ✓✗ mol dm^{-3} s^{-1} ✗ ②

  (ii) Because the rate is proportional to concentration, when concentration is multiplied by 1.5 the rate is 4.5×10^{-5} mol dm^{-3}. ✓ ③

  (iii) At a higher temperature the particles have more energy ✓ so they move faster and collide more, meaning they react faster. ✗✗ ④

Examiner commentary

① To measure rate you need to take a measurement that changes over time – if time is not measured then this will reduce the marks so 'colorimetry' without time is not enough for a mark.

② Proportion is a good method for working out rates for first order reactions so gains a mark.

③ When significant figures are requested in bold print, then only these are accepted, so he loses a mark for an answer to 2 significant figures.

④ Although there are more collisions at a higher temperature, this is not the main factor, it is the energy of the collisions that makes the main difference.

Tom achieves 3 out of 9 marks.

Seren's answer

(a) Since there is a change in colour we can use colorimetry to measure the colour over time. ✓ The change in the number of molecules of gas can be tracked using pressure measurements at constant volume. ✓ ①

(b) (i) k = Rate ÷ $[N_2O_5]$ = 3.00×10^{-3} ÷ 4.00×10^{-5}
= 7.50×10^{-3} ✓✓ s^{-1} ✓

  (ii) Using the rate equation, rate = $7.50 \times 10^{-3} \times 6.00 \times 10^{-3}$ = 4.5×10^{-5} mol dm^{-3}. ✓ ②

  (iii) When the temperature is increased, particles have more kinetic energy ✓. This means that when the particles collide, the collisions have more energy so more of the collisions have energy above the activation energy ✓ meaning that there are more frequent successful collisions. ✓ ③

Examiner commentary

① Two methods are suggested and although time is only mentioned once, this is enough to gain both marks

② Both calculations are correct.

③ An answer is terms of activation energy and the frequency of successful collisions gains all the available marks.

Seren achieves 9 marks out of 9.

Q&A 26

Rate equations and mechanisms

Hydrogen peroxide (H_2O_2) in solution decomposes to release oxygen gas when in the presence of iodide ions. The equation for this process is:

$$2H_2O_2 \rightarrow 2H_2O + O_2$$

The reaction was repeated using several different concentrations of hydrogen peroxide and iodide ions. The results of these experiments are given below.

Concentration of H_2O_2 / mol dm^{-3}	Concentration of I$^-$ / mol dm^{-3}	Initial rate / mol dm^{-3} s^{-1}
2.00×10^{-2}	2.00×10^{-3}	4.82×10^{7}
4.00×10^{-2}	2.00×10^{-3}	9.64×10^{7}
4.00×10^{-2}	4.00×10^{-3}	1.93×10^{8}

(a) Calculate the orders of the reaction with respect to H_2O_2 and iodide ions and hence write a rate equation for this reaction. [3]

(b) State the function of the iodide ions in this reaction and explain your reasoning. [2]

(c) Two proposed mechanisms for this reaction are given below as mechanism A and mechanism B. State and explain which of these two mechanisms is consistent with the rate equation you have found in part (a). [2]

$H_2O_2 \rightarrow H^+ + HO_2^-$ $HO_2^- + HO_2^- \rightarrow 2HO^- + O_2$ $H^+ + I^- + HO^- \rightarrow H_2O + I^-$ *Mechanism A*	$H_2O_2 + I^- \rightarrow HOI + HO^-$ $HOI + H_2O_2 \rightarrow H_2O + O_2 + HI$ $HI + OH^- \rightarrow H_2O + I^-$ *Mechanism B*

Tom's answer

(a) Doubling the concentration of H_2O_2 doubles rate so the order is 1. ✓ Doubling the concentration of iodide doesn't double the rate so the order is 0. ✗ ①
Rate = k[H_2O_2] ✓

(b) Iodide is needed for the reaction to occur. ✗ ②

(c) Mechanism A as it only has H_2O_2 in the first step and this is the slowest step. The rate equation only has H_2O_2 in it so it matches. ✓✗ ③

Seren's answer

(a) H_2O_2 is first order ✓, and iodide is first order ✓, giving a rate equation of:
Rate = k[H_2O_2][I$^-$] ✓ ①

(b) The iodide increases the rate even though it is not part of the overall equation ✓ so the iodide acts as a catalyst ✓. ②

(c) Mechanism B as it has one H_2O_2 molecule and one iodide as the reactants in the rate determining step which matches the two compounds in the rate equation, and both of these are first order. ✓✓ ③

Examiner commentary

① This is correct for H_2O_2 but incorrect for I$^-$; however, the orders are correctly used to produce a rate equation so this gains a mark even though it is not the correct answer.

② This tells us nothing and gains no mark.

③ This answer follows from the rate equation and gives a reason so gains a mark but the reason is insufficient for the second mark.

Tom achieves 3 out of 7 marks

Examiner commentary

① Both orders are calculated correctly, giving an overall rate equation.

② Catalysts will appear in the rate equation but will not appear in the chemical equation so this answer is correct.

③ The correct answer with a full reason gains both marks.

Seren achieves 7 out of 7 marks.

Enthalpies of formation

Sodium hydride, NaH, is a solid that reacts with water. The synthesis of the compound from the elements sodium and hydrogen is an exothermic process:

$$Na\ (s) + \tfrac{1}{2} H_2\ (g) \rightarrow NaH\ (s) \qquad \Delta H^\theta = -57\ kJ\ mol^{-1}$$

(a) Give the name of the enthalpy change above. [1]

(b) Use the enthalpy change above, and those listed in the table below to calculate the enthalpy of lattice formation for sodium hydride, NaH. [3]

Equation	Enthalpy change / kJ mol^{-1}
$Na\ (s) \rightarrow Na\ (g)$	109
$H_2\ (g) \rightarrow 2H\ (g)$	436
$Na\ (g) \rightarrow Na^+\ (g) + e$	494
$H\ (g) + e \rightarrow H^-\ (g)$	−72

(c) When NaH is added to water, the following reaction occurs:

$$NaH\ (s) + H_2O\ (l) \rightarrow NaOH\ (aq) + H_2\ (g)$$

Calculate the number of moles of NaH and hence the volume of hydrogen gas produced under standard conditions when 1.2g of NaH is added to water. [2]

[1 mole of gas occupies 24 dm^3 under standard conditions]

Tom's answer

(a) Enthalpy of formation of NaH. ✓①

(b) $\Delta H = 109 + 436 + 494 - 72 + \Delta H_{Latt}$ ✗
  $-57 - 109 - 436 - 494 + 72 = \Delta H_{Latt}$ ✓
  $\Delta H_{Latt} = -1024\ kJ\ mol^{-1}$ ✓②

(c) $M_r(NaH) = 23 + 1.01 = 24.01$
  Moles (NaH) = 1.2 ÷ 24.01 = 0.05 ✗
  Volume gas = 0.05 × 24 = 1.2 dm^3 ✓③

Examiner commentary

① (a) is correct.

② Tom has not noticed that the equation given for 436 kJ mol^{-1} involves 2H so this must be halved. He gains the marks available for the remainder of the method.

③ Tom correctly calculates the moles of NaH and the volume of gas, but misses a mark as he has overtruncated the moles of NaH.

Tom achieves 4 out of 6 marks.

Seren's answer

(a) Enthalpy of formation for NaH (s). ✓①

(b) $-57 = 109 + \tfrac{1}{2} \times 436 + 494 - 72 + \Delta H_{Latt}$ ✓
  $-57 - 109 - 218 - 494 + 72 = \Delta H_{Latt}$ ✓
  $\Delta H_{Latt} = -806\ kJ\ mol^{-1}$ ✓②

(c) $M_r(NaH) = 23 + 1.01 = 24.01$
  Moles (NaH) = 1.2 ÷ 24.01 = 0.04998 ✓
  Volume gas = 0.04998 × 24 = 1.20 dm^3 ✓③

Examiner commentary

① (a) is correct.

② Seren has worked out the stages that need to be combined to make the overall process, and rearranges the equation correctly to gain full marks.

③ Seren correctly calculates the moles of NaH and uses this to calculate the volume of gas.

Seren achieves 6 out of 6 marks.

Q&A

28

Enthalpy and entropy

The equation below shows the complete combustion of liquid methanol.

$$CH_3OH \text{ (l)} + 1\tfrac{1}{2}O_2 \text{ (g)} \rightarrow CO_2 \text{ (g)} + 2\,H_2O \text{ (l)}$$

(a) Use the enthalpy changes of formation listed in the table below to calculate the enthalpy change of this reaction. [2]

	Standard enthalpy change of formation / kJ mol^{-1}
CH_3OH (l)	−239
CO_2 (g)	−394
H_2O (l)	−286
O_2 (g)	0

(b) Explain why the enthalpy change of formation of O_2 (g) is zero. [1]

(c) (i) The entropy change of this reaction is −81 J K^{-1} mol^{-1}. Use this value to calculate the Gibbs free energy for this reaction at 298 K. [2]

(ii) Explain how the answer to (c)(i) allows us to decide whether the reaction is feasible. [1]

Tom's answer

(a) ΔH = products − reactants
$\quad = -394 - 286 - 239$ ✗
$\quad = -919$ kJ mol^{-1} ✗ ①

(b) The enthalpy of formation is the enthalpy change from the element so it is zero for oxygen. ✗ ②

(c) (i) $\Delta G = \Delta H - T\Delta S$ ✓ $\quad = -919 - 300 \times -81$
$\quad = 23381$ kJ mol^{-1} ✗ ③

(ii) The value is positive so the reaction is not feasible. ✓ ④

Examiner commentary

① Incorrect as Tom has forgotten to include the factor of two for the two water molecules, and the value for methanol should be positive.

② The details here are insufficient as there is no reference to standard state.

③ He has forgotten to convert the entropy to kJ, so he loses a mark, but gains a mark for a correct expression for ΔG.

④ A mark is awarded as the answer is consistent with the value obtained in part (i)

Tom achieves 2 out of 6 marks.

Seren's answer

(a) ΔH = products − reactants
$\quad = -394 - 2 \times 286 - (-239)$ ✓
$\quad = -727$ kJ mol^{-1} ✓ ①

(b) The enthalpy of formation is the enthalpy change when a substance is formed from its elements in their standard states, in this case O_2 (g). Since there is no change the enthalpy change is zero. ✓ ②

(c) (i) $\Delta G = \Delta H - T\Delta S$ ✓ $\quad = -727000 - 300 \times -81$
$\quad = -702700$ ✗ ③

(ii) The reaction is feasible. ✗ ④

Examiner commentary

① Calculated correctly and gains both marks.

② The explanation is full and detailed and so gains the mark.

③ This is correctly calculated; however, the answer given has no units, and this is penalised as we assume kJ mol^{-1} as this is the standard unit for ΔG.

④ This answer gives no explanation so gains no mark.

Seren achieves 4 out of 6 marks.

&Q A

29

Using Gibbs free energy

When calcium nitrate is heated, the solid decomposes according to the equation below.

$$2\ Ca(NO_3)_2\ (s)\ \rightarrow\ 2\ CaO\ (s) + 4\ NO_2\ (g) + O_2\ (g)$$

(a) The standard enthalpy change, ΔH^θ, for the reaction is 740 kJ mol^{-1}. Use this value and the data in the table to calculate the standard enthalpy of formation, ΔH_f^θ, for calcium nitrate, $Ca(NO_3)_2$. [2]

	ΔH_f^θ / kJ mol^{-1}	S^θ / J mol^{-1} K^{-1}
$Ca(NO_3)_2$	?	193
CaO	−635	40
NO_2	34	240
O2	0	205

(b) Use the values given to calculate the entropy change ΔS^θ for this reaction in J mol^{-1} K^{-1}. [2]

(c) State the relationship between Gibbs free energy, enthalpy and entropy [1]

(d) Use the expression for Gibbs free energy to calculate the minimum temperature, in K, required for decomposition of calcium nitrate. [3]

Tom's answer

(a) $\Delta H = 2 \times -635 + 4 \times 34 + 0 - 2 \times ?$ ✓
  $740 - 2 \times -635 - 4 \times 34 = 2 \times ?$
  Answer = 937 kJ mol^{-1} ✗ ①

(b) ΔS^θ = products − reactants
  $= 2 \times 40 + 4 \times 240 + 205 - 2 \times 193$ ✓
  $= 654$ J mol^{-1} K^{-1} ✓②

(c) $\Delta G = \Delta H - T\Delta S$ ✓ ③

(d) When the reaction is able to happen then ΔG must become negative, and it becomes negative at zero. ✓
  $\Delta G = 740 - T \times 654 = 0$ so $T \times 654 = 740$ ✗
  $T = 740 \div 654 = 1.1\ ^\circ C$ ✗ ④

Examiner commentary

① Tom has the correct idea but makes an error in rearrangement of the equation which loses a mark.

② ③ Both correct.

④ Starts correctly; however, he forgets to convert between J and kJ so both entropy and enthalpy can be used together. He finally gives the answer in the wrong temperature units.

Tom achieves 5 out of 8 marks.

Seren's answer

(a) $740 = (2 \times -635) + (4 \times 34) + 0 - (2 \times \Delta H_f)$ ✓
  $740 - (2 \times -635) - (4 \times 34) = -(2 \times \Delta H_f)$
  $2 \times \Delta H_f = -1874$
  Answer $= -937$ kJ mol^{-1} ✓

(b) $\Delta S^\theta = (2 \times 40) + (4 \times 240) + 205 - (2 \times 193)$ ✓
  $= 654$ J mol^{-1} K^{-1} ✓

(c) $\Delta G = \Delta H - T\Delta S$ ✓

(d) The reaction starts to be feasible when $\Delta G = 0$ so $\Delta H - T\Delta S = 0$ giving $T = \Delta H \div \Delta S$ ✓
  We need to use the same units for ΔH and ΔS so $\Delta H = 740,000$ J mol^{-1}. ✓
  $T = \Delta H \div \Delta S = 740000 \div 654 = 1131$ K ✓

Examiner commentary

Seren shows her ability to undertake calculations competently. All of Seren's answers are correct, with all units used correctly.

Seren achieves 8 out of 8 marks.

Equilibria

One stage in the production of nitric acid involves the oxidation of ammonia, which is a reversible reaction as shown below.

$$4 \, NH_3 \, (g) + 5 \, O_2 \, (g) \rightleftharpoons 4NO \, (g) + 6 \, H_2O \, (g)$$

(a) Write the expression for the equilibrium constant, K_p, for this reaction. [1]

(b) The values for all the partial pressures are typically given with units of Pa. Give the units, if any, of K_p for this reaction. [1]

(c) A platinum/rhodium catalyst is used in the industrial process. State the effect, if any, of adding a catalyst on the position of this equilibrium. [1]

(d) This reaction is usually undertaken under a pressure of 500 kPa. State and explain the effects, if any, of increasing the pressure on the position of equilibrium and the rate of the forward reaction. [4]

Tom's answer

(a) $K_p = \dfrac{P_{NO} \times P_{H_2O}}{P_{NH_3} \times P_{O_2}}$ ✗ ①

(b) There will be no units. ✓ ②

(c) Catalysts affect the rate the forward and reverse reactions, so these cancel out. ✗ ③

(d) The reaction is faster at a higher pressure ✓ ✗ and it produces more product. ✗✗ ④

Examiner commentary

① Tom has forgotten the powers so loses the mark.

② This mark is given as the answer follows from the expression given in part (a) even though this is incorrect.

③ This is the correct idea but doesn't answer the question completely so doesn't gain the mark.

④ The effect on rate is correct, but the effect on the equilibrium is not. Neither are explained so this limits the mark available.

Tom achieves 2 out of 7 marks.

Seren's answer

(a) $K_p = \dfrac{P_{NO}^{4} \times P_{H_2O}^{6}}{P_{NH_3}^{4} \times P_{O_2}^{5}}$ ✓ ①

(b) Units will be Pa. ✓ ②

(c) Catalysts affect the rate but not the position of equilibrium. ✓ ③

(d) The reaction is faster at a higher pressure ✓ as the particles collide more ✗. The equilibrium will try to decrease the pressure according to Le Chatelier's principle so it will go to the side with fewer gas molecules, which shifts the equilibrium to the left. ✓✓ ④

Examiner commentary

①–③ Exactly what was expected for the marks.

④ The effect on rate is correct, but the explanation is not sufficient. The effect on the equilibrium is correct with a clear explanation so she gains both marks here.

Seren achieves 6 out of 7 marks.

Q&A 31

Equilibrium calculations

Nitrogen dioxide, NO_2, exists in dynamic equilibrium with dinitrogen tetroxide, N_2O_4,

$$2NO_2 \text{ (g)} \rightleftharpoons N_2O_4 \text{ (g)} \qquad \Delta H = -57.2 \text{ kJ mol}^{-1}$$

(a) Write an expression for the equilibrium constant, K_p, for this reaction. [1]

(b) State and explain the effect of increasing the temperature on the value of K_p. [2]

(c) At a temperature of 373 K, the partial pressure of a pure sample of NO_2 was 3.00×10^5 Pa. When the mixture was allowed to reach equilibrium, the partial pressure of the remaining NO_2 was 2.81×10^5 Pa.

Calculate the value of K_p, stating its units. [3]

Tom's answer

(a) $K_p = \dfrac{P_{N_2O_4}}{P_{NO_2}^{\,2}}$ ✓ ①

(b) The reaction is exothermic so increasing temperature shifts equilibrium in the direction that is endothermic ✗ so the value of K_p is increased. ✗ ②

(c) Amount of NO_2 converted $= 3.00 \times 10^5 - 2.81 \times 10^5$
$= 0.19 \times 10^5$ Pa

so $P_{N_2O_4} = 0.19 \times 10^5$ Pa ✗

$K_p = 0.19 \times 10^5 \div (2.81 \times 10^5)^2 = 2.40 \times 10^{-7}$ ✓✗ ③

Examiner commentary

① Correct.

② There is not enough detail for the first mark – Tom doesn't give the direction that the equilibrium will shift, and the effect on K_p is incorrect.

③ The calculation includes a common error. He has forgotten that one N_2O_4 is made from 2 NO_2 molecules. He uses this value correctly to calculate K_p but gives no units so loses a mark.

Tom achieves 2 out of 6 marks.

Seren's answer

(a) $K_p = \dfrac{P_{N_2O_4}}{P_{NO_2}^{\,2}}$ ✓ ①

(b) The reaction is exothermic so increasing temperature shifts equilibrium to left as this direction is endothermic ✓ so the value of K_p is decreased as the amount of product is decreased. ✓ ②

(c) Amount of NO_2 converted $= 3.00 \times 10^5 - 2.81 \times 10^5 = 0.19 \times 10^5$ Pa

$P_{N_2O_4} = 9.5 \times 10^3$ Pa ✓

$K_p = 9.5 \times 10^3 \div (2.81 \times 10^5)^2 = 1.20 \times 10^{-7}$ ✓

Units $= Pa^{-1}$ ✓ ③

Examiner commentary

① Correct.

② A full explanation gains both marks.

③ Seren has noticed that one N_2O_4 is made from 2 NO_2 molecules, so there will be half as much N_2O_4 as the NO_2 that is used up. She uses this value correctly to calculate K_p and its units.

Seren achieves 6 out of 6 marks.

Q&A

32

Acids and pH

Methanoic acid, HCOOH, is a weak acid.

(a) Explain what is meant by the term *weak acid*. [1]

(b) Write an expression for K_a for this acid. [1]

(c) The pH for a solution of methanoic acid is 2.35.
  (i) Calculate the concentration of H+ ions in this solution. [2]
  (ii) The concentration of the acid in solution is 0.12 mol dm⁻³.
       Calculate the K_a of methanoic acid, giving its units. [2]

(d) When methanoic acid reacts with ammonia, it undergoes the following reaction:

$$\text{HCOOH (aq)} + \text{NH}_3 \text{ (aq)} \rightleftharpoons \text{NH}_4^+ \text{ (aq)} + \text{HCOO}^- \text{ (aq)}$$

Identify every molecule that behaves as a base in this equation, explaining your answer. [2]

Tom's answer

(a) A weak acid is one that dissociates partially. ✗ ①

(b) $K_a = \dfrac{[\text{H}^+][\text{HCOO}^-]}{[\text{HCOOH}]}$ ✓ ②

(c) (i) pH = − log[H⁺] ✓ ③
    [H⁺] = 4.47 × 10⁻³ mol dm⁻³ ✓

   (ii) K_a = 4.47 × 10⁻³ ÷ 0.12 ✗ ④
        K_a = 3.73 × 10⁻² mol dm⁻³ ✓

(d) Bases are substances that react with acids so the only base in this case is NH₃. ✗✗ ⑤

Examiner commentary

① Tom fails to indicate what is meant by the 'acid' part of 'weak acid'.

②–③ Both correct.

④ Calculated incorrectly but the units are correct.

⑤ Tom fails to indicate both bases clearly, or explain why there are two bases.

Tom achieves 4 out of 8 marks.

Seren's answer

(a) A weak acid is one that releases H⁺ in a reversible reaction so not all the possible H⁺ are released. ✓ ①

(b) $K_a = \dfrac{[\text{H}^+][\text{HCOO}^-]}{[\text{HCOOH}]}$ ✓

(c) (i) pH = − log[H⁺] ✓
    [H⁺] = 4.47 × 10⁻³ mol dm⁻³ ✓

   (ii) K_a = (4.47 × 10⁻³)² ÷ 0.12 ✓
        K_a = 1.67 × 10⁻⁴ ✗ ②

(d) This is a reversible reaction, and both directions are acid-base reactions. In the forward reaction, NH₃ is the base as it accepts a H⁺ from the HCOOH ✓ and in the reverse reaction HCOO⁻ acts as a base as it accepts a H⁺ from the ammonium. ✓ ③

Examiner commentary

① Seren shows an understanding of both 'weak' and 'acid'.

② (b) and (c) are stated and calculated correctly, but a mark is lost for the lack of units.

③ Seren has realised that acid-base reactions include both a base as a reactant and conjugate base in the products and explains this clearly.

Seren achieves 7 out of 8 marks.

Bases and buffers

(a) Sodium hydroxide is a strong base. Calculate the pH of a solution of sodium hydroxide of concentration 0.25 mol dm^{-3}.
[The ionic product of water, K_w, is 1.00×10^{-14} mol^2 dm^{-6} at 298 K] *[2]*

(b) A buffer solution was made by adding 19.6 g of sodium 3-chloropropanoate, CH_2ClCH_2COONa, to 1.00 dm^3 of 3-chloropropanoic acid, CH_2ClCH_2COOH, of concentration 0.100 mol dm^{-3} at 298 K.
(K_a for 3-chloropropanoic acid = 7.94×10^{-5} mol dm^{-3} at 298 K)

  (i) Calculate the concentration of the sodium 3-chloropropanoate in mol dm−3. *[1]*

  (ii) Calculate the pH of the buffer solution at 298 K. *[2]*

  (iii) Explain how this aqueous solution of 3-chloropropanoic acid and sodium 3-chloropropanoate can act as a buffer solution when a small amount of acid or alkali is **separately** added to it. *[3]*

Tom's answer

(a) pH = −log(0.25) = 0.6 ✗✗ ①

(b) (i) M_r = 36 + 35.5 + 4.04 + 32 + 23 = 130.54
    Concentration =19.6 ÷ M_r ÷ 1=0.150 mol dm^{-3} ✓

(ii) [H$^+$] = $\dfrac{K_a \times [CH_2ClCH_2COOH\,]}{[CH_2ClCH_2COO^-]}$

  [H$^+$] = $7.94 \times 10^{-5} \times 0.100 \div 0.150 = 5.29 \times 10^{-5}$ ✓ ②
  pH = − log (5.29×10^{-5}) = 4.3 ✓

(iii) The 3-chloropropanoic acid dissociates to release H$^+$ ions:
$CH_2ClCH_2COOH \rightarrow CH_2ClCH_2COO^- + H^+$ ✗
Adding base will react with the H$^+$ to neutralise it keeping the pH constant. ✗ If you add acid the molecules will react with the CH_2ClCH_2COONa and remove them. ✗ ③

Examiner commentary

① Tom has forgotten that pH relates to [H$^+$] and has incorrectly used [OH$^-$], so gains no marks for part (a).

② Correctly calculated gaining full marks.

③ Shows a lack of understanding of how buffers work. The key concept is the equilibrium and how adding acid and base affects this.

Tom achieves 3 out of 8 marks.

Seren's answer

(a) K_w = [H$^+$] × [OH$^-$]
  [H$^+$] = $1.00 \times 10^{-14} \div 0.25 = 4.00 \times 10^{-14}$ mol dm^{-3} ✓
  pH = −log [H$^+$] = −log 4.00×10^{-14} = 13.4 ✓

(b) (i) M_r = 36 + 35.5 + 4.04 + 32 + 23 = 130.54
    Concentration = 19.6 ÷ M_r ÷ 1=0.150 mol dm^{-3} ✓

(ii) K_a = $\dfrac{[H^+][A^-]}{[HA]}$

so [H$^+$] = K_a × [HA] ÷ [A$^-$]
[H$^+$] = $7.94 \times 10^{-5} \times 0.100 \div 0.150 = 5.29 \times 10^{-5}$ ✓
pH = − log (5.29×10^{-5}) = 4.28 ✓ ①

(iii) The sodium 3-chloropropanoate dissociates completely:
$CH_2ClCH_2COONa \rightarrow CH_2ClCH_2COO^- + Na^+$
The 3-chloropropanoic acid sets up an equilibrium:
$CH_2ClCH_2COOH \rightleftharpoons CH_2ClCH_2COO^- + H^+$ ✓
Adding acid means that the equilibrium will shift to the left, removing H$^+$ ✓. Adding base will shift the equilibrium in the opposite direction. ✗ ②

Examiner commentary

① Seren has correctly calculated the answers to all parts.

② Seren's explanation of how a buffer works is correct but she lacks enough detail on the effect of adding a base to gain the final mark.

Seren achieves 7 out of 8 marks.

Q&A 34

Titrations and buffers

The graph shows the change in pH that occurred when aqueous sodium hydroxide of concentration $0.1\ mol\ dm^{-3}$ was added to $25\ cm^3$ of aqueous ethanoic acid of concentration $0.1\ mol\ dm^{-3}$.

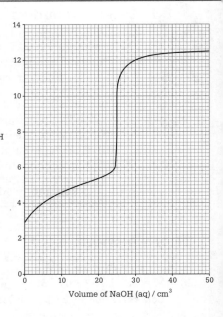

(a) Select, from the table below, the name of an acid-base indicator which is suitable for this titration, giving a reason for your choice. *[2]*

Indicator	Range
Tropaeolin OO	1.3–3.0
Bromocresol green	3.8–5.4
Thymolphthalein	8.3–10.5
Tropaeolin O	11.1–12.7

(b) Sodium ethanoate does not have a pH value of 7.
 (i) State, giving a reason, the pH of aqueous sodium ethanoate. *[2]*
 (ii) Explain why the pH of aqueous sodium chloride is 7 whilst an aqueous solution of sodium ethanoate is not. *[2]*

Tom's answer

(a) Thymolphthalein is the right indicator ✓ as it falls in the straight part of the graph. ✗ ①

(b) (i) 9.0 ✓ as this is the endpoint of the titration. ✗ ②

 (ii) Sodium ethanoate releases ethanoate ions when dissolved in water. The ethanoate ions set up an equilibrium by reacting with H^+ which reduces the concentration of these giving a pH above 7. ✓ ③

Examiner commentary

① Tom has the correct idea; however, he needed to discuss the vertical region not the straight region, and refer to the pH range of the indicator.

② This has the correct pH but 'end point' refers to the indicator colour change and he needed to discuss the formation of the sodium ethanoate in solution.

③ Tom gains the mark for the sodium ethanoate, but he doesn't refer to the sodium chloride.

Tom achieves 3 out of 6 marks.

Seren's answer

(a) Thymolphthalein would work as an indicator ✓ as the range lies completely within the vertical section of the graph. ✓

(b) (i) At the vertical section of the curve, the solution contains only sodium ethanoate. ✓ The midpoint of the vertical section is 9.0 ✓ which gives the pH of this salt.

 (ii) Sodium ethanoate solution contains ethanoate ions, whilst NaCl releases chloride ions. Ethanoic acid is a weak acid, so ethanoate ions remove H^+ ions in a reversible reaction to form ethanoic acid. ✓ HCl is a strong acid so chloride will not remove H^+ to form HCl. ✓

Examiner commentary

Seren's answers are clear and complete gaining full marks. She answers concisely but has ensured she answers each part of each question to gain the highest possible marks.

Seren achieves 6 out of 6 marks.

Quickfire answers

CH4 Analysing and Building Molecules

① Only red light can be reflected. If there is no red light to be reflected the flower appears black.

② The colours of the spectrum that are not green – red, orange, blue, etc.

③ It absorbs green and therefore it is purple.

④ It contains two carbon atoms and both these carbon atoms are aldehyde groups.

⑤

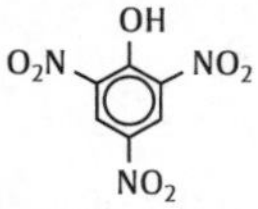

⑥

⑦

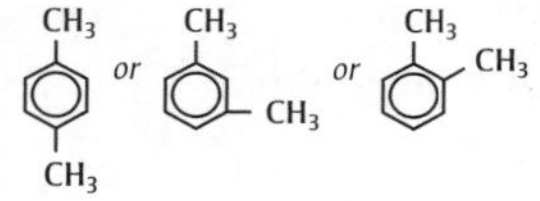

⑧

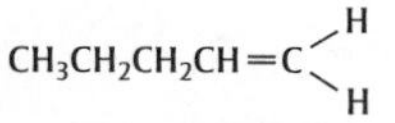

$CH_3CH_2CH_2CH = C$

It has two atoms that are the same, bonded to one carbon of the double bond.

⑨

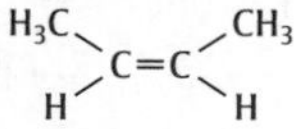

⑩

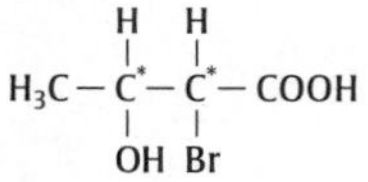

⑪ 12.3 g

⑫ 76.4%

⑬ Pentan-3-ol

⑭

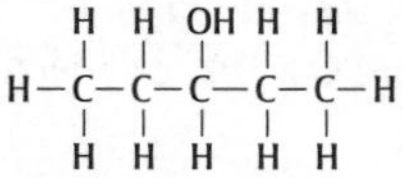

⑮

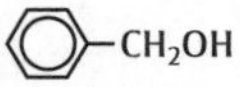

⑯ (a) hex-2-ene

(b) methanal

(c) propane-1,2-diol

(d) butanone

⑰ Pentan-3-one

⑱ About 162°C

The boiling temperature rises by about 20°C for each additional carbon atom.

⑲ It has strong hydrogen bonds between molecules and will also hydrogen bond with water.

⑳ Pentane

㉑ 2-Methylpropanoyl chloride

㉒ 125.6 g

㉓ 3-Methylbutanenitrile

㉔ (i) Add KCN

(ii) Add $LiAlH_4$ in ethoxyethane

㉕ Pentylamine

㉖ $Cl(CH_2)_6Cl$

㉗ $C_{12}H_{11}N_3$

㉘ Effervescence

㉙

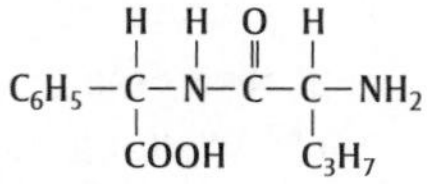

$C_6H_5 - C - N - C - C - NH_2$

㉚

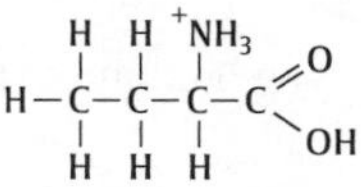

㉛ Effervescence

㉜ Use a different column

㉝ Otherwise the mixture would dissolve in the solvent in the beaker

㉞ (i) $LiAlH_4$

(ii) Concentrated H_2SO_4

㉟ (i) Water/steam (and phosphoric acid catalyst)

(ii) Acidified potassium dichromate

㊱ X is chloromethane or bromomethane

Y is ethanenitrile

㊲

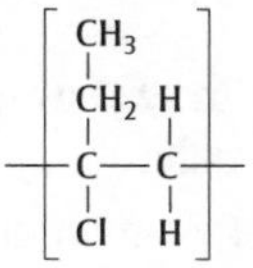

㊳

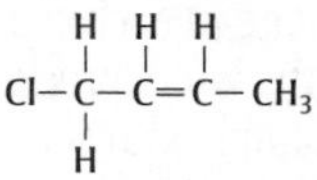

$Cl - C - C = C - CH_3$ or the *E*-isomer

1-chlorobut-2-ene

CH5 Physical and Inorganic Chemistry

① S_8: S = 0 Fe^{3+}: Fe = +3   NaCl: Na = +1
H_2O: O = −2 F_2O: O = +2 CaH_2: H = −1
$AlCl_4^-$: Al = +3   NaOCl: Cl = +1 $NaIO_3$: I = +5
MnO_4^-: Mn = +7

②

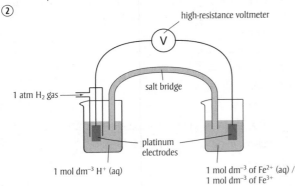

high-resistance voltmeter
V
salt bridge
1 atm H_2 gas
platinum electrodes
1 mol dm^{-3} H^+ (aq)   1 mol dm^{-3} of Fe^{2+} (aq) / 1 mol dm^{-3} of Fe^{3+}

③ a) EMF = 0.34 − (−0.76) = 1.10V
   b) EMF = 0.77 − (−0.76) = 1.53V

④ Chlorine has a more positive E^θ value than bromine, which shows that chlorine is a stronger oxidising agent than bromine and can oxidise bromide to bromine.

Iodine has a less positive E^θ value than bromine so it cannot oxidise the bromide to Br_2.

⑤ $2 MnO_4^- + 16 H^+ + 10 Cl^- \rightarrow 2 Mn^{2+} + 8 H_2O + 5 Cl_2$

⑥ Moles MnO_4^- = 0.200 × 21.40 ÷ 1000 = 0.00428 moles.

Moles Fe^{2+} = 0.00428 × 5 = 0.0214
Mass Fe = 0.0214 × 55.8 = 1.194g
% by mass = 1.194 ÷ 1.252 x 100 = 95.4%

⑦ Concentration of Cu^{2+} = 0.248 × 30.25 ÷ 25.00 = 0.300 mol dm^{-3}

⑧ As you go down group 4 the stability of the +2 oxidation state increases due to the inert pair effect. Carbon is stable as +4 so CO will be easily oxidised making it a reducing agent.

Lead is stable in the +2 oxidation state so PbO won't be able to reduce other substances as it is stable.

⑨ Addition of sodium hydroxide to colourless solutions of each will produce a white precipitate in each one. If excess sodium hydroxide is added, the white precipitate remains in the magnesium nitrate sample, but the precipitate dissolves for lead(II) nitrate to leave a colourless solution. The difference is because lead is an amphoteric metal and magnesium is not.

⑩ $NaHSO_4$

SO_2 – pungent, acidic gas
S – yellow solid
H_2S – rotten egg smell

⑪ Ti: $1s^2 2s^2 2p^6 3s^2 3p^6 3d^2 4s^2$
Co: $1s^2 2s^2 2p^6 3s^2 3p^6 3d^7 4s^2$
Cr^{3+}: $1s^2 2s^2 2p^6 3s^2 3p^6 3d^3$
Ni^{2+}: $1s^2 2s^2 2p^6 3s^2 3p^6 3d^8$

⑫ Cu^{2+} (aq) + 2 OH^- (aq) → $Cu(OH)_2$ (s)
Fe^{3+} (aq) + 3 OH^- (aq) → $Fe(OH)_3$ (s)

⑬ (i) Measure the pressure (at constant volume) over time.
(ii) Measure the volume (at constant pressure) over time.
(iii) Measure colour change by colorimetry over time.

⑭ Rate = 0.046 ÷ 10 = 0.0046 mol s^{-1}

⑮ (i) Second order; units of k = mol^{-1} dm^3 s^{-1}
(ii) First order; units of k = s^{-1}

⑯ Rate = k $[N_2O_5][H_2O]$

⑰ $C_4H_9Br + OH^- \rightarrow C_4H_9OH + Br^-$

⑱ ΔS = 73 + 214 − 136 = 151 J K^{-1} mol^{-1}

⑲ ΔH = (−416) + (−394) − (−1131) = 321 kJ mol^{-1}

⑳ ΔG = ΔH − TΔS = 321 − 300 × (151÷1000) = 275.7 kJ mol^{-1}

㉑ T = ΔH ÷ ΔS = 321,000 ÷ 151 = 2126 K

㉒ $$K_p = \frac{P_{NO}^4 \times P_{H_2O}^6}{P_{NH_3}^4 \times P_{O_2}^5}$$

㉓ If we increase the temperature then according to Le Chatelier's principle the equilibrium will shift to the endothermic direction. This is a shift to the left, increasing the partial pressure of SO_2 and O_2 and decreasing the partial pressure of SO_3. This will decrease the value of K_p.

㉔ pH = - log (0.015) = 1.82

㉕ $[H^+]$ = 6.31 × 10^{-4} mol dm^{-3}

㉖ $[H^+]$ = 2.38 × 10^{-3} mol dm^{-3} giving a pH of 2.55

㉗ K_a = 2.0 × 10^{-9} mol dm^{-3}

㉘ $[H^+]$ = 3.33 × 10^{-14} giving a pH of 13.5

㉙ $[H^+]$ = 8.0 × 10^{-6} giving a pH of 5.1